HAUNTED BOSTON

Famous Phantoms, Sinister Sites, and
Lingering Legends

Retold by Taryn Plumb

Globe
Pequot

Guilford, Connecticut

*To the sick, sordid, and imaginatively gruesome minds
who have spun horror and fear: Clive Barker, Wes Craven,
Lucio Fulci, Stephen King, Edgar Allan Poe, Bram Stoker
(just the tip of the gates of hell, so to speak).
Thank you for igniting the fire of my imagination.
Because of you, there are monsters.*

Globe
Pequot

An imprint of Rowman & Littlefield

Distributed by NATIONAL BOOK NETWORK

Copyright © 2016 by Rowman & Littlefield

British Library Cataloguing in Publication Information Available

Library of Congress Cataloging-in-Publication Data

Names: Plumb, Taryn , 1981- author.
Title: Haunted Boston : famous phantoms, sinister sites, and lingering legends / retold by Taryn Plumb.
Description: Guilford, Connecticut : Globe Pequot, an imprint of Rowman & Littlefield, 2016. | Includes bibliographical references. | Description based on print version record and CIP data provided by publisher; resource not viewed.
Identifiers: LCCN 2016000184 (print) | LCCN 2015044883 (ebook) | ISBN 9781493024933 (ebook) | ISBN 9780762771813 (pbk.)
Subjects: LCSH: Haunted places—Massachusetts—Boston. | Ghosts—Massachusetts—Boston.
Classification: LCC BF1472.U6 (print) | LCC BF1472.U6 P59 2016 (ebook) | DDC 133.109744/61—dc23
LC record available at http://lccn.loc.gov/2016000184

∞™ The paper used in this publication meets the minimum requirements of American National Standard for Information Sciences—Permanence of Paper for Printed Library Materials, ANSI/NISO Z39.48-1992.

CONTENTS

CONTENTS

CONTENTS

CONTENTS

INTRODUCTION

> Behind every man now alive stand thirty
> ghosts, for that is the ratio by which the
> dead outnumber the living.
> —Arthur C. Clarke, *2001: A Space Odyssey*

Beantown. The Hub. (Why thank you, Oliver Wendell Holmes!) The Walking City. The Cradle of Liberty (although Philadelphia also jostles for that dignified moniker).

Cultured, iconic, educated, diverse, fast-paced, a nerve center of ideas, architecturally rich, historically gilded.

Boston (or, to mimic the local colloquialism, "Baahstin") has many names, even more attributes: It's home to nearly three dozen colleges, an incubator for innovation, and its residents are headstrong and proud (especially when it comes to their sports teams); the numerous events that occurred over its 385 years of existence are pivotal not only to its own history, but to that of the country, and, ultimately, the world.

And with history, come ghosts. Centuries' worth of them.

Much like artifacts, they linger—serving as mysteries, reminders, cautionary tales; readily revealing themselves, coyly being coaxed out over time, or content to remain abstruse and unseen for hundreds of years. Boston and its surroundings are plentiful with specters, apparitions, and ghouls both benign and spiteful, along with other legends and lore of the unexplained, the unidentified, the eerie, and the outright terrifying.

Founded in 1630 just a decade after the momentous *Mayflower* landing, Boston has long been a city of secrets and firsts—it was where patriotism was fomented with such events as the 1770 Boston Massacre and the Boston Tea Party in 1773, literally igniting with the first volley of shots and ensuing initial casualties of the American Revolution in adjacent Lexington and Concord. It was the location of the first regularly issued newspaper, the first state constitution, the first subway, the first telephone, the first schools for African Americans and for the blind. It also bred the likes of Whitey Bulger and the still (positively) unidentified "Boston Strangler" (or "stranglers"); played unfortunate host to the tragic 2013 Boston Marathon bombing and the infamously accident-prone and money-devouring Big Dig.

Much like other turbulent historic cities, generations of Bostonians have lived through times of corruption and success, plenty and pain, revolution and reinvention.

As Mark Twain once remarked of their experience and studiousness, "In New York, they ask, 'How much money does he have?' In Philadelphia, they ask, 'Who were his parents?' In Boston they ask, 'How much does he know?'"

It is a city (and an area at large) where the bygone and the present are infused—and indeed, where the past is so prevalent that it can't possibly be left behind or forgotten.

Nor can its ghosts—rebellious and persistent, a trait they share with both their ancestors and their descendants, they endure.

Part 1

AN EERIE INVESTIGATION

Now I know what a ghost is. Unfinished business, that's what.

—Salman Rushdie

As long as we have been able to walk upright and form thoughts, humans have striven to make contact with the things we have no words for, that which we have been so long unable to comprehend.

Come along, explore the unknown, in the cold and dark far beyond twilight.

Chapter 1

A Chilly (and Chilling) Evening at the Veasey Estate in Groveland

It's 9:05 p.m. A January night.

A penetrating chill bites even gloved fingers raw and stiffens joints to rusty hinges; Venus lingers in the sky as the moon tarries in its arrival.

Cresting a hill in the small north-of-Boston town of Groveland, a rambling building—its main structure a little over a century old but with a hodgepodge of newer sections tacked on here and there over the decades—sits hulking and dark against the cold.

But not empty.

Navigating its dim passageways, empty and echoing halls, and various rooms where antique furniture stands in bulky silhouette, a team of researchers outfitted with a cadre of cameras, recorders, and meters is here hoping to bridge the chasm between our tangible world and the spectral one.

Members of the Massachusetts paranormal group the New England Ghost Project, they begin their investigation in the estate's living room—giant fireplace at center set with stones carved and stippled by the nearby Merrimack River; decor of Oriental rugs and colorful glass lamps—that serves as the centerpiece of the forty-seven-and-a-half acre town-owned Veasey Memorial Park.

The flag outside slaps in protest against the frigid wind; the boiler below hums in a constant and conscientious battle against nature's pervasive draft. The team members hold their equipment aloft, sweeping it across the darkened space. The floorboards grouse as the visitors walk around like moving shadows; their voices are disembodied and reverberating in the dark; the lights from their equipment shine like tiny red eyes.

"Do you feel anything?" Ron Kolek, founder of the New England Ghost Project, asks the gathered assembly.

"As I'm sitting here, I feel dizzy," replies self-described medium Lesley Marden.

"Spinny dizzy?" Kolek volleys.

"Like when you've had too much to drink dizzy," Marden clarifies.

This bit of information is copied back to the control room by walkie-talkie. A click and a hiss and the reply, "Got it."

Recorder running, Jim Stonier, a self-identified specialist in electronic voice phenomena (EVP), asks of unseen attendants, "Anyone in here who would like to communicate?"

After a moment or two, he continues. "We just want to make contact with you. We mean you no harm. We come with the utmost respect."

Pause. "What is your name?"

Another beat. This time, Kolek: "Are you a male?"

After a few more simple questions, they rewind the recording, play it back. The deliberate halts between their questions are filled in: a rhythmic sound, low and deep and grating, like the thrumming of tired-out machinery.

Not a name or a positive answer to the gender question—but clearly, inexplicably, something.

WARMHEARTED WRAITHS

The Veasey estate, named for the early twentieth-century mill owner who built it, is indicative of the nature of the ghosts of the Boston area. From illustrious historical sites to spots ever so obscure (even encompassing just mere square feet of land), specters and apparitions, whether malevolent or harmless, don't discriminate. They are ubiquitous throughout the region—only fitting for an area so resonant with history.

Veasey, although one of greater Boston's lesser-known haunted locales, remains one of its most active and enigmatic.

Full-bodied apparitions have been sighted there, and various images and sounds have been captured in encounters both sought after and chance. Kolek, a doubter-transformed-believer after experiencing a close brush with death, has explored Veasey on numerous occasions, and describes each and every time as different, unpredictable.

"You have no idea what to expect," says the resident of the town of Dracut during a recent, on-site investigation, who has also written books about his various expeditions plumbing the ghostly realm, hosts radio shows about the metaphysical, and teaches Ghost Hunting 101 classes. "You just go in being open, and whatever happens, you react to it."

Erected between 1909 and 1910, the estate—initially a bungalow but now encompassing a chapel, hall, suite, mill, and green room—served as a summer home for wealthy industrialist Arthur D. Veasey. Built on a hill overlooking a pond, it was constructed in the Arts and Crafts style, which succeeded the embellished Victorian era of architecture, and embraced simplicity, practicality, unobtrusiveness, and locally sourced materials and labor.

A quintessential self-made man and fervent outdoorsman, Veasey started out driving carriages for successful businessman Benjamin Hale around 1873 at age nineteen; intelligent and ambitious, he worked his way up through Hale's company and eventually bought out his boss. His three-building operation, erased with time, was the once thriving Groveland Mills. Workers there produced fabric and wool, initially for blankets for the Union Army, later for seats for newfangled machines known as automobiles being manufactured by Henry Ford.

But by the 1930s, the mill equipment became outdated, and the buildings were dismantled. After Veasey passed, his family sold the property, which changed hands several times before it came into the possession of an order of Italian Catholic nuns, the Little Missionary Sisters of Charity, in the 1950s. Their initial mission was to establish a novitiate on the property, a proving ground for prospective nuns. But with the tempestuousness of the 1960s and the defunding of state asylums in the latter half of the twentieth century, they turned their attention to the care of the mentally ill. That began with women displaced by Danvers State Hospital, who were set up in dorm rooms the nuns built in the bungalow's larger rooms. Over the years, they also added an east wing that encompassed a large and small chapel, a dining hall and function hall, as well as a swimming pool and a cottage that hosted visiting priests and, later, hospice patients.

Finally, in 1996, eighty-five-plus years after it was erected, the town of Groveland purchased the property.

Given the estate's altruistic history, the phantoms that are said to inhabit it are believed to be mostly benign. "The nuns did so much care and worshipful loving here for so many years, I really feel that they infused the place," Kolek says while standing in the group's makeshift command center on a harshly cold Saturday night in mid-January. "I get such a feeling of well-being when here. I don't think there's anything scary here."

Still, that's not to say that run-ins with the supposed local spirits aren't shocking.

In particular, many visitors to the property have witnessed two nunnish-looking" women—one big, one little. Kolek came upon them—or, rather, they upon him—one night when he was house-sitting the property when it was on the real estate market. As he was watching TV, they abruptly entered the room, startling him, and walked right through a wall. The same ethereal duo has been seen hovering in the kitchen area.

Then there have been less palpable presences—for instance, when park event manager Dorna Caskie stayed over one night with her two children, they were all startled awake at 3 a.m. "I felt like I was in a room full of very excited and very happy children," she says from a spot in the kitchen, a set of property keys jangling from her elbow. It was "absolutely electric and very profound."

ETHEREAL INSPECTION

Kolek and his team hope for something similarly intense on this winter night.

A little after 7 p.m., they show up in the dark parking lot, a caravan of cars and SUVs, the building a stark contour against the white slope of snow.

Bustling with a rhythm of routine, the crew of a half dozen lugs in large black cases of equipment, unreels and runs long strings of electrical cords along hardwood and linoleum, positions cameras (four in total) in various rooms, and sets up a temporary control station of several monitors, all the while communicating via walkie-talkie.

As Kolek explains, they always run without lights, and always at night, because the atmosphere is much quieter and there are fewer (human) bodies around. Also, "some people believe that the veil between the two realms is thinner at night," he explains.

Ultimately, as he describes, ghost hunting—whether you're an earnest believer, a cynic, or agnostic—has a unique methodology involving an array of technology, measured calculations, deduction, analysis, and a keen ability to discern between what are believed to be "real" encounters or just mere flukes.

With a degree in environmental science and a background working for the space program and Raytheon, he was an unlikely convert to paranormal research—he was, as he describes, "the ultimate skeptic" for most of his life. That all changed nearly twenty years ago, when he accidentally maimed his left hand with a table saw, severing his middle finger and the tip of his thumb. They were reattached in a six-hour operation—but during the process, he suffered a pulmonary embolism and was taken to the intensive care unit. After that near-death experience, he became intrigued with the celestial world.

Now, "I call myself a dumb psychic," he says of his various brushes with the "body impaired," as he jokingly refers to ghosts. "I don't really try; things just come to me."

With a shrug: "We're all our own instruments."

Scattered around the building, members of the team make use of theirs to take "baseline" scans. Some employ handheld temperature gauges and meters that pick up on electromagnetic fields; others record markedly different impressions.

Marden, of Laconia, New Hampshire—a small city tucked along the shore of Lake Winnipesaukee—uses her perceptions to feel out the varying intensities of power across the rooms. With her is Karin Ruck of the nearby town of Boxford (who doesn't call herself a medium, per se, but claims to have "sensitivities").

"As a whole, this place has a nice energy. It's kind of inviting," reflects Marden, documenting her responses on a digital device. Describing herself as "aware of the things that people couldn't see for as far back as I can remember," she reports "a lot of different energies" in the turn-of-the-twentieth-century building.

Inside the great room: a sense of the 1940s. Within the kitchen: something having to do with head trauma. Elsewhere: a grazing touch of the walls yields an aura of "sickness," or corroded arteries.

In the basement, meanwhile, both she and Ruck identify a male energy and an unmistakable path, trodden over the decades, passing from the entry door to the kitchen.

"It's just this tunnel of energy," Marden considers. She takes a few steps and pauses. "Then it kind of ends here."

Back upstairs, in a small room raised a few steps and now used by the local chapter of the Veterans of Foreign Wars (VFW), Marden stops, looking around, one hand on her hip.

"Nervous energy," Ruck whispers, as much to herself as to her spirit-seeking partner.

"I feel like I have to pace," Marden says. She begins to do so, then blurts, "Male."

Back down in the control room, Kolek ensures every-thing is ready, scanning the four-way, split-screen monitor, securing cables, testing meters and walkie-talkies.

All is prepped. Soon, the lights go off, one by one. The examination begins.

In the one-time living room, the half dozen or so gath-ered make note of various energies. Gravitating to one of the corners near the fireplace, Marden says she senses a man with a mustache and dark hair, then announces "flash!" as she takes a photo. The space is illuminated in a quick burst of light, its visitors and their surroundings suspended behind temporarily strained eyes as a sort of real-life photo-graphic negative when the dark descends once more.

"I feel someone watching us, male," Kolek says, striding to and fro.

Marden muses as she walks in her own pendulous way, "I get a sensation in my legs."

She starts, "Ooh! The corner's kind of funky."

"Isn't it?"

"That's more than residual."

They move along to the adjacent room, a clock dust-ily ticking the seconds along, rocking chairs creaking back and forth as the spectral detectives take their seats. Marden reports a "female energy"; Ruck a headache on the left side of her head.

The radio squeals with static. Apparently, as they are informed, the monitors show the distinctive image of a woman. Stonier addresses one member of the group: "Well—there's someone sitting next to you."

Later, while on a lone vigil in the kitchen, Kolek sees what he describes as light anomalies (or unexplained, but clearly discernible, moving beams of light). He also captures what he believes is a ghost trying to make contact.

In a recording, he poses a question: "There have been reports of a female spirit here—are you here?"

The response occurs in just a split second—it could be a guttural, breathy "No!" A whoosh of clothing. A gruff brush against the sensitive microphone.

For hours, the group continues in its exploration, pausing in each room for anywhere from a minute to several, all the while taking pictures, capturing sound and video—then moving on to the next.

By 12:30 a.m., the moon finally having made its appearance, rays glancing off the bright snowy hill leading down from the bungalow, the team repacks their equipment, hauls it back out, loads up their cars.

As they go, the building sits silent and brooding atop its hill, clinging to its secrets.

Part 2

THE CENTER OF IT ALL

It's not called "the Hub" for nothing.

Since the nickname was co-opted and abbreviated from an initially satirical characterization made by Oliver Wendell Holmes Sr. in 1858—the poet-doctor compared the city's egocentricity to that of "all other considerable, and inconsiderable places"—Boston has been a center of intellectualism, ingenuity, and ideas.

And, also, spirits. As with their non-cadaverous counterparts who work, live, study, innovate, and create here, ghosts of all types are particularly active in the thrumming heart of the city.

Chapter 2
The Boston Common

It's April 1895. The cusp of a new and vibrant century. Advancements all across the spectrum—from medicine, to transportation, to manufacturing, to technology—are fundamentally revolutionizing day-to-day life.

Down on the historic Boston Common, a massive project is underway to construct the country's first subway—ultimately culminating in nearly two miles of tunnels cutting seventeen feet underground, and costing an estimated five million dollars, as reported by the *Boston Globe*. It is an exciting and anticipated development, and spectators from all across the city gather in crowds to catch glimpses of the massive undertaking.

But as the earth is excavated to make way for what will eventually be the Boylston Green Line T stop—workers tackling trenches in sections, horses continuously hauling away cartful by cartful of fill, dust clogging the spring air—more than dirt and rocks are revealed.

Inexplicably, human remains are mixed in among the detritus: skulls in various states of completeness, a variety of bones—some as frail and dry as twigs—fragments of rotted clothing, clumps of hair that unforgiving time diminished to the consistency of hay.

It is a grisly and disturbing find, and one that ultimately hints at a dark past lingering—quite literally—just beneath the surface of this centuries-old historic, pastoral landscape.

With progress, come casualties. Every civilization is built upon the pain of the suffering. In Boston, one of the country's oldest and most historic cities, the story is no different.

Take a walk today along Boston Common—the United States' first city park—and you'll find it teeming with a riot of life: sunbathers, picnickers, shade-seekers reading or lounging beneath stately maples and oaks that silently have watched this city transform with the passing centuries; historical reenactors, musicians; flying Frisbees, the enticing aroma of sweet and salty indulgences wafting from push carts.

But this conviviality conceals a macabre history of persecution, intolerance, pain, and untimely death. And, as a result, the fifty-acre green space that attracts both tourists and locals of the living variety is said to be a roaming ground for a number of aggrieved, mistreated, listless—and also a couple of decidedly benign—spirits.

COMMON HAUNTS

Imagine this space as it was roughly 450 years ago—relatively unperturbed, wild, referred to by the natives as "Shawmut." Civilization begins to encroach in the late 1620s: Anglican clergyman William Blaxton—often spelled "Blackstone" in more contemporary times—lays claim to it after emigrating from Europe in the late 1500s on a religious mission. He settles in the area that is now the tony Beacon Hill neighborhood, effectively becoming Boston's first known permanent European resident. He builds a cabin, plants the first apple orchard, and uses the land that is today's Common as a grazing area for his livestock.

Time brings more European settlers, and the Puritans soon dominate the area, which they establish as the Massachusetts Bay Colony in the mid-1600s. As their burgeoning population begins to swell the borders of their settlement, they turn to Blaxton, purchasing fifty acres for communal purposes.

Thus, the Boston Common is established in 1634.

As the years pass, its use changes with the times; it is a public grazing land at first, then a camp for soldiers during the English occupation and the bloody Revolutionary War, and, most notoriously, as the Puritans enact their strict and inflexible rule, the setting for innumerable public hangings and the site of a massive, unmarked burial ground.

For nearly two hundred years, the large green space serves as a prolific and bloody execution site. The Puritans, particularly, do not discriminate with the noose—anyone from lesser criminals to murderers, pirates, Native Americans, Quakers, and accused witches were strung up by the neck. Initially, the thick branches of an enormous elm with an umbrella-like canopy serves as the fateful end for many a traitor, malcontent, or would-be revolutionary—as well as many of the falsely accused or those simply born to the wrong city or the wrong era. Later, hangmen make use of traditional gallows.

The deathly setup is finally disassembled in 1817, as prevailing opinion begins to view public execution as cruel and unusual. In 1876, as if for further confirmation of the changing times, the infamous hanging tree is toppled in a storm—perhaps no longer able to bear the burden of the countless souls it has taken?—and its former location is today commemorated by a simple weathered plaque set in the ground.

But until then, as neck by neck is slung up, the gruesome—and decidedly unsanitary—practice is to leave the dead bodies dangling on display for an indefinite amount of time, one reason being to serve as a deterrent for those contemplating malicious deeds. If family or friends—or perhaps just an empathetic stranger—did not come by the cloak of night to cut the corpse down and bury it in an unidentified grave on the common, it was eventually removed and dumped unceremoniously in the Charles River.

But some believe they linger still. Visitors have reported seeing ghostly apparitions swaying in the Common's trees—accompanied in some cases by the eerie creak of rope rubbing against wood.

One of the most famous victims of the gallows—whose story also serves as a testimony to the double standard of the "religious freedom" sought by European immigrants to the new land—was Quaker Mary Dyer.

In the mid-1600s, Puritans denounced Quakers as heretics in the Massachusetts Bay Colony. But Dyer, openly violating the Puritans' rigid laws, freely interpreted the Bible and preached to fellow Quakers and others on the Boston Common and elsewhere in New England's early settlements. For her brash actions, she was banished from the Colony on at least three occasions—relocating to Quaker-tolerant Rhode Island—but she unflaggingly continued to return to Boston to spread her beliefs. The Puritans responded by threatening her with the noose, and one well-circulated story tells how she was quite literally given a last-minute reprieve—purportedly when she was on the Common's gallows with a rope cinched tight around her neck.

Still, the Puritans didn't stop with mere intimidation; their tactic was pure vilification. Governor John Winthrop, upon hearing that Dyer had given birth to a deformed, stillborn baby girl, ordered the infant body exhumed and brought it forth as "evidence" of the pious Quaker's purported heresy. Famously calling it a "monster," he described the infant, as recounted by Nicholas Goodwin in *Spooky Creepy Boston*, as having a face but no head or forehead; two mouths, each with "a piece of red flesh sticking out"; four horns, "hard and sharp" over its eyes; "sharp pricks and scales" covering its breast and back; its navel and belly reversed with its back and hips; apelike ears on its shoulders; and, instead of toes, "on each foot three claws, like a young fowl, with sharp talons." The unfortunate malformation of an innocent child—but for superstitious and devil-fearing Puritans, a terrifying prospect indeed.

Exasperated by her relentless persistence—blasphemy, as they would portray it—the Puritans ultimately came through on their threats, hanging Dyer on June 1, 1660. With her well-recounted refusal to repent at the gallows, she secured a status in history as a religious martyr.

Today, she is commemorated with a statue in front of the State House; seated on a bench in a conservative dress and bonnet, hands clasped in her lap, she bears a contemplative countenance.

But it's said that her convictions are carried on in more than her bronze likeness. Over the years, there have been varied reports of a mysterious woman in colonial dress wandering around the Common, in some cases weeping. For the harsh and unrelenting treatment of her people? For her malformed unborn child? Only the supposed specter, if she should chose to tell her tale, could say for sure.

THE DISCARDED ONES

All of us would like to be remembered in some way or another after our deaths—whether through our children, our work, or an enduring legacy we helped to build. Many, though, have never been given that chance.

The Common, in addition to claiming the lives of untold guilty and innocent at its gallows, has served another ghastly purpose: a mass, catchall grave for society's nameless unfortunates, including criminals, the homeless, destitute, and infirm, as well as felled patriot and British soldiers. And what should serve ultimately as a site of enduring respite, its abutting cemetery, Central Burying Ground, also has an inordinate share of displaced, disturbed, anonymous, and hidden dead.

Many of them might have stayed at peace—in unmarked graves or otherwise—had it not been for the slow advance of civilization.

In 1836, during a project to connect Boylston and Tremont Streets in downtown Boston, workers cut off a portion of the perimeter of Central Burying Ground, effectively eliminating several graves. It's said that some of those original inhabitants were left where they were and keep their final rest beneath the ensuing walkway and mall that runs alongside the cemetery. Others, according to the city, were relocated to a tomb on the western edge of the burial ground.

Meanwhile, in 1895, as workers made their laborious progress beneath Boston's streets for the pioneering subway system—known to today's travelers simply as the T—they began to hit upon gruesome artifacts. Work was halted; the eminent Samuel Abbott Green, a doctor and one-time Boston mayor, was brought in for analysis. "This incident was but the beginning of the discovery of other remains which continued daily in considerable numbers for several weeks," Green wrote in a July 1895 letter to the Boston Transit Commission.

Acknowledging that the discovery was not altogether unanticipated due to the previous disruption during the excavation of the Boylston mall, he noted that various pieces of the dug-up skeletons were "so incomplete" that it was "impossible now to say with any exactness how many different persons they represented." In some cases, the fragments were so small that "if found elsewhere would not have been recognized as belonging to the human frame," he reported. All were diligently collected—and, where possible, corresponding parts of the same body amassed in a box together. In just two instances, remains from tombs of the Tuttle and Lowell families were identified and taken away by representatives, according to Green.

Meanwhile, a line of buried tombs that he extrapolated were used for the reception of bones unearthed during the Boylston mall project sixty years earlier were found in a range of conditions, from "fair and good" to "almost entirely destroyed." Coffins were decayed, brick arches caved in, and bones "much decomposed." "So confused were the contents that it was impossible to find out the number of original internments," Green wrote.

All told, he estimated that all the remains—previously disturbed, not previously disturbed, and "lying in confusion"—totaled 1,000 unidentified bodies from various burials over the years.

But the interruption of their last sleep didn't stop there; beyond their disinterment, looting spectators purportedly further disturbed the bodies by confiscating macabre souvenirs of bones, hair, and other artifacts abandoned to time.

The gruesome find—coupled with accidental deaths, gas line leaks, and frequent flooding—ultimately prompted the pastor of Park Street Church adjacent to the Common to deem the subway an "infernal hole" and an "un-Christian outrage," according to the *Boston Globe*. It also fueled fears that subterranean digging would release long-abolished diseases. Following the horrifying discovery, the *Boston Post* fanned public angst with the sensational headline "Hideous Germs Lurk in the Underground Air," accompanied by a grotesque illustration of a hairless, fanged, two-headed parasite with a globular, featureless body and numerous grasping pincers. It was dubbed the "subway microbe."

The discovered remains were eventually buried in a mass grave in the northwest corner of Central Burying Ground and marked fittingly with a large, featureless stone with a simple, concise inscription: "Here were re-interred the remains of persons found under the Boylston Street mall during the digging of the subway, 1895." As Green noted, a spot was discovered in the cemetery where the remains could be re-interred without, in turn, disturbing even more adjoining graves.

Boston's fourth cemetery, established in 1756, Central is the ultimate resting place of an estimated 1,600 men, women, and children—although that number would be difficult to corroborate based on the disparate amount of tombs. Scattered, lichen-covered, and tilted askew by time, they do not betray each and every one of their eternal occupants.

Among the notables resting within the burial ground's depths are William Billings (considered the architect of American choral music) and Gilbert Stuart (painter of iconic presidential portraits, although he, buried in an unmarked grave, remains forever anonymous). They lie alongside numerous patriot and British soldiers, foreigners who died while in Boston, and Irish Catholic immigrants whose graves, reflecting their long-repressed status, are simply identified with the word "stranger."

Restless for their multitude of reasons, many of the Common's known and unknown dead are said to make their presence known—and some are not at all shy about it. Similarly, it should be noted that flowers—which serve as a harbinger of sorts to final rest—are not plentiful upon the common proper (although they do, however, flourish in the adjacent public garden).

Visitors to Central Burying Ground have described a prevailing feeling of being watched, or a general sense of unease and discomfort (not altogether uncommon for those walking among the domains set aside for the dead). Others have reported seeing shadowy figures sidling alongside trees—perhaps disquieted victims of the gallows? Some witnesses have gone so far as to claim sensory contact: a poke to the back, a brush against the shoulder, the groping of a hand in the pocket rattling change and keys. On one or two occasions, others have even sworn they were harshly grabbed from behind—with no one there to confront when they whirled around to identify their brusque attacker.

In the 1970s, retired dentist Jim McCabe had an even more intimate, oft-described run-in. As he was passing by, he recalled encountering a curious girl; with stringy red hair and an ashy and unhealthy complexion, she was dressed in a filthy, out-of-style garment. Unsettled, he turned away from her—but the mischievous, omnipresent apparition appeared immediately in front of him again and again, no matter which way he faced. As he hurried on, the ghoulish girl supposedly further taunted him by stealthily removing his car keys from his pocket—then returning them and abruptly disappearing.

Meanwhile, down below in the bowels of the city, the subway tunnels are said to have at least one of their own roving specters. A British soldier, dressed in full redcoat attire and holding a musket, has been seen on several occasions standing on the tracks. A phenomenon experienced in the deep hush of the morning, it is purportedly an initiation of sorts for new T drivers.

Elsewhere on the Common, less menacing spirits haven't been hesitant to show themselves. Particularly, two women in Victorian-era dress—strolling pleasantly, chatting inaudibly, seemingly enjoying the day—have materialized among the masses, then suddenly disappear as soon as addressed or acknowledged by the living.

So ultimately it should be emphasized that, just as history doesn't come blemish-free, not all those who linger are lost.

Chapter 3

You Can Check Out Any Time You Like. . . .

THE OMNI PARKER HOTEL

Just the hurly-burly nature of their business makes hotels a haven for paranormal happenings—the constant influx and departure of people with a diverse array of backgrounds from all over the world; of different ages; at different stages of life and success; coming, going, starting out, washing up, in love, in lust, seeking revenge, asking forgiveness, closing deals, losing them, preparing for the future with a streak of hope or stubbornly stuck in the past.

For more than 150 years, Boston's historic Omni Parker House, just a short distance from the Common at the base of Beacon Hill on School Street, has catered to a panoply of clientele, both living and not, merely passing through or settling in for a permanent stay.

Like many young men starting fresh in a new city, hotel founder Harvey Parker came to Boston in 1825 with only a dream and a dollar in his pocket. Thirty years later, transformed by persistence and hard work, the real estate mogul saw the opening of his long-anticipated design: a magnificent five-story, Italianate-style hotel. Officially checking in its first guests in 1855, it attracted the rich and famous, historical legends and notorious alike. According to the upscale resort, its register contains such eminent names as Ulysses S. Grant, John F. Kennedy, Franklin Delano Roosevelt, Babe

Ruth, Ted Williams, James Dean, and Judy Garland (as well as contemporary notables such as Colin Powell, Red Sox slugger David "Big Papi" Ortiz, former Boston governor Deval Patrick, and actor/director Ben Affleck). Meanwhile, a group of the nineteenth century's most influential and well-known authors and philosophers, including Charles Dickens, Nathaniel Hawthorne, Henry David Thoreau, Ralph Waldo Emerson, John Greenleaf Whittier, Henry Wadsworth Long-fellow, and Oliver Wendell Holmes, formed what they called the "Saturday Club," choosing the Parker House as the site of their monthly meetings.

More infamously, assassin John Wilkes Booth was a guest just a week prior to dealing the fatal wound to President Abraham Lincoln at the Ford Theater 450 miles south in Washington, D.C. Portentously, he was seen practicing his aim at a Boston shooting range. Polarizing human rights activist Malcolm X was a once a waiter in the hotel's kitchen, and Vietnamese communist revolutionary Ho Chi Minh also spent time working there as a baker.

Ultimately, though, perhaps the Parker House's most famous guests are the ones who have extended their welcomes far beyond the normal check-out times.

The hotel's third floor is undeniably active; it was there that Dickens and Longfellow stayed while in town—and it was there that at least two notable deaths occurred. In 1876, stage actress Charlotte Cushman, a known lesbian at a time when homosexuality was very much taboo, died of pneumonia in her third-floor suite—and is said to keep up her prima donna antics today. Down the hall, in notorious room 303, a liquor salesman is said to have overdosed on whiskey and barbiturates while there as a guest in 1949. Both employees and patrons alike have reported his abiding presence; a ghostly form lying naked on the floor, accompanied by the overpowering, nostril-stinging aroma of alcohol, has shocked many an onlooker. Because purported sightings were so frequent and the story so lurid, the hotel shuttered the infamous room and converted it into a maid's closet. But that doesn't mean encounters have ceased—guests still report emanating sounds of drunken, hiccupy laughter coming from the storage room, as well as the sweet earthy scent of whiskey.

The hotel elevator also seems beckoned to the floor, routinely halting at its threshold empty, and without any summons. Similarly, a mirror from Dickens's oft-frequented room is believed to be somehow enchanted or imbued with the celebrated storyteller's spirit. (It was in front of it that he was said to practice his orations.) Moved to the end of a hallway on the second floor, flanked by two lamps and a period rotary telephone, the large, arching, wood-framed looking glass is said to bear Dickens's reflection for those who stare into its depths long enough (a phenomenon that has also been accompanied by condensation—as if from the warm breath of someone standing close).

But it's not just the third floor that experiences all the otherworldly action. There and elsewhere throughout the hotel, guests have reported voices and footsteps without origin, lights and other fixtures turning on and off by themselves, doors opening and closing of their own volition, ominous shadows looming along the walls, and large, floating orbs making their way down hallways.

And Parker himself also reportedly retains a presence at his namesake hotel. Following his death at age seventy-nine in 1884, various guests and staff began to recount their sightings of a stately, well-dressed gentleman wandering the halls, as if taking appraisal of one of his grandest achievements.

In a more jarring—but not altogether unpleasant—experience, overnight visitors have also claimed to have been woken from the midst of sleep by a shadowy man in their room; easygoing and pleasant, he genuinely takes an interest in their lodgings, asking about their stay and what could be done to enhance it.

Ultimately, it brings a whole new meaning to the term "room service."

Chapter 4
A Few Fleeting Haunts

CHARLESGATE HALL

It's perhaps one of the country's most haunted spaces—and there isn't much of the darkly sinister or paranormal variety of occurrences that haven't reportedly taken place here. Built in 1891 as a hotel, it passed through various stages as a residence hall for Boston University and Emerson College, a rooming house, and finally condominiums. Although its otherworldly activity has since dropped to a din, it was once described as a "vortex of evil," according to self-described paranormal journalist Sam Baltrusis in *Ghosts of Boston: Haunts of the Hub.*

Murders, satanic rituals, suicides, elevator "accidents," and Mafia hits in soundproof rooms are just some of the dark events reported. With Ouija boards—and, no doubt, illicit substances in wide use—students also described hidden rooms, precipitous temperature fluctuations, a cacophony of unexplained noises, and other unpleasantries such as blankets being ripped off in the midst of sleep. Encounters with the ghost of a little girl were also described, as well as a roaming "man in black," and an evil, unknown, basement-bound creature ominously dubbed "Fury."

SHELTON HALL

Eugene O'Neill is said to keep a permanent presence at this Boston University (BU) dorm, initially built as one of the first posh Sheraton Hotels in 1923. The writer, who brought the world such celebrated works as *The Iceman Cometh* and *The Hairy Ape*—lugubrious and footed in the realism of suffering—lived in room 401 of the hotel with his wife Carlotta until his death in 1953. According to Baltrusis, his last salty words were "Born in a hotel room and goddammit, died in a hotel room." The year after his passing, BU purchased the building, honoring him by naming the floor "Writer's Corridor." But the playwright's long day's journey into night didn't end there—the area where he once spent his final days has been plagued by shadowy figures, phantom knocks, strange voices in the dark, unexplained gusts of wind, flickering lights, windows opening and closing at their own command, and, much like the Parker House, an elevator that seems persistently drawn by an unseen presence—over and over again—to the fourth floor.

HUNTINGTON THEATRE

The stage is a place where dreams are made and dashed—so it only makes sense that it would also be a drawing point for idle souls. Established in 1923 and still in operation through a partnership with BU, sightings here have included a gentleman (thought to be a former city mayor) lounging in a back row during rehearsals, shadowy figures on catwalks and above the stage, a hovering "lady in white" whispering encouragements to nervous cast and crew members, and a diaphanous entity known as "the Sentry," who is believed to be a protective spirit.

BOSTON ATHENAEUM

This independent library is the site of a famous, recurrent run-in by Nathaniel Hawthorne with the specter of Rev. Thaddeus M. Harris. A lifetime member of the Athenaeum, the author claimed to have first seen the reverend's specter in 1842—reading his own obituary. For days, his apparition continued to appear, sitting unperturbed to read the newspaper. Hawthorne, who wrote about the encounter in his short story "The Ghost of Dr. Harris," later quipped that he hesitated to address the ghost because the two had never been properly introduced in human life.

Part 3

UNSETTLED ISLES

Dotted along Boston Harbor are dozens of islands: close in, far out, mere specks swallowed by the waves, promontories rising above them. For centuries, as civilization has made its embellishments along the coast of this historic maritime city, they have served as beacons, forts, and deterrents to the malicious prowlers of the ocean, private land, refuges, and leisure spots.

And each and every one of them, in their turn, has a story to tell.

Chapter 5

Fort Warren's "Lady in Black"

The impressions in the snow were dainty and small, beginning suddenly and ending just as abruptly—as if their bearer had alighted down from the sky for just the briefest of moments.

Unbelievable on an island populated solely by men—and practically impossible on an enclave that required passage across a treacherous and frigid harbor in the midst of winter.

The soldiers, muskets in hand, stared down in disbelief.

This, as they were to learn later, was their first purported encounter with the infamous "Lady in Black."

One of Boston's most legendary phantoms, she is said to relentlessly roam the grounds of Fort Warren, located on George's Island seven miles off the Boston coast. Making her presence known in a variety of wicked and insidious ways, she is believed to be eternally enacting vengeance for the grievous treatment of her and her long-lost husband—and also perhaps letting loose her unquenched rage and sorrow over her own liability in the tragedy.

Hers is a tale of true love, sacrifice, heartbreak—the unfortunate ending to most great love stories—and, ultimately, a deep and enduring revenge.

It all began as the embers—which had been smoldering, smoking, and threatening to spark for decades—finally ignited into the Civil War. In 1861, a young southerner, Andrew Lanier (or Samuel in some versions of the story) was summoned to fight for the Confederates in the conflict that pitted North against South, blood against blood, friend against friend.

Primed for battle in a raucous and uncertain time, little could he suspect that his untimely death would not come at the hands of his sworn enemies.

After enlistment, he secured a short leave, swiftly riding his steed home to the tiny enclave of Crawfordville, Georgia. There, he proposed to his young sweetheart—like her beau, her precise first name is lost to time and legend, although some say it was Melanie—and the ceremony took place on June 28, 1861. With just forty-eight hours together as husband and wife, the couple celebrated with a brief honeymoon and by intoning their favorite song, the old English ballad "Drink to Me Only with Thine Eyes," as told by Holly Mascott Nadler in *Ghosts of Boston Town: Three Centuries of True Hauntings.*

Back on duty as the war accelerated, the young groom was stationed at Roanoke Island on the Outer Banks of North Carolina. But soon, Northern forces stormed the isle, Lanier was knocked unconscious and captured, and, along with numerous other Confederate soldiers, was shipped north to Fort Warren.

Dating to the 1830s, the pentagon-shaped garrison was crafted of granite from the abundant quarries from Quincy to the south, according to noted maritime historian and author Edward Rowe Snow. Its outer parapet was sixty-nine feet above the tide marker, and its walls were eight feet thick.

Over the course of the war, according to Rowe Snow, it was the prison camp of more than 1,000 Confederate soldiers. Known—perhaps in stories that were over embellished—for its bleak and filthy conditions and pitiless treatment of prisoners, it was referred to grimly as the "corridor of dungeons." Rats were particularly unruly and brash, with tails said to be as thick around as a man's finger, and a penchant for gnawing through everything (including, in one anecdote retold by Rowe Snow that can only prompt a revolting shiver, the hair of a soldier that had been recently slicked down with barber's oil).

Still, despite the conditions and strict regulations at the fort, Lanier was able to secure a letter to his bride hundreds of miles south. Clearly despondent, lonely, and in fear for his life, he described his capture, the wretched imprisonment at the will of the Yankees, and his despair that he would never live to see her or the outside of the fort's confines ever again.

Determined and swift thinking, his young bride didn't hesitate; she chopped off her hair, concealed herself in men's clothing, secured a pistol, and sought safe passage to the North. Eventually, she set down in Hull—just south of Boston and with a clear sight line of George's Island a mile offshore—and found refuge with a Southern sympathizer.

Then, she plotted.

For days on end, ceaseless and resolute, she stood onshore with a telescope, intimately familiarizing herself with the fort's barracks, grounds, stone walls, and guard booths. Finally, on a frigid, stormy night nearly three months after receiving her husband's disheartening correspondence, she took action. Getting a row across the harbor from her host, they made a treacherous trek through pelting rain, searing lightning and cloaking mist. She landed ashore on the island outside the thick walls of the fort, clutching a bundle carrying her pistol and a short-handled pickax.

Timing her movements around the circuits of patrolling soldiers whose regimented routines she had memorized, she scaled the fort wall, sprinted across the grounds as her Yankee adversaries' backs were turned, and approached a window secured with thick bars.

Suddenly unsure of how to alert her husband—she hadn't been able to send a return message, after all—she resorted to singing a few bars of their song: "Drink to me only with thine eyes / And I will pledge with mine," according to Mascott Nadler's account.

Pausing, she listened.

Nothing.

Alarmed, anxious, she suddenly let loose a long, shrill whistle.

Listened again.

Straining to hear through the howling night, she finally heard the return volley of a whistle from above. It was quickly followed by a bedsheet, twisted into a ropelike form, unfurling from the window. With short time before the sentries returned, she took hold of it and quickly sidled up the wall to the window. Several hands gripped her from inside, helping her ease her small frame through a narrow opening in the bars.

She tumbled into a dungeon, duskily lit by kerosene lanterns, the eyes of many weary prisoners both awed and heartened by this tenacious young woman standing before them—dressed in men's clothing, bedraggled, shivering, out of breath, soaked through by the storm.

Soon, she once again found herself in her lover's arms— the long-anticipated reunion.

But with time short and the soldiers anxious for freedom, she was hastened off to a central area where a committee of prisoners was plotting various methods of escape. Their main plan was to begin to dig a tunnel beneath the fort until they emerged onshore and met with a prearranged schooner. But with her arrival, they changed their tactic, deciding instead to dig inward, breaking through into the parade grounds, where they could access the arsenal and arm themselves. From there, they would seek retribution: Their plan was to overpower the Union soldiers and turn the fort's cannons onto Boston.

Over the course of the next several weeks, they set about their work—digging with Mrs. Lanier's pickax, planning and replanning as they encountered obstacles, working in the depths of night and the bowels of morning. A rotating crew of men excavated while others loaded as much dirt as possible into sacks made from their shirts, then dumping it out windows. Meanwhile, a larger mound that accumulated outside the tunnel was trampled down and lounged upon whenever captors were close.

Finally, after long hours of toil and scant sleep, the pickax sliced through into the open air—and pinged off the fort's stone wall.

A night watchman heard the unmistakable clank, sounding an alarm. Commander Justin Dimmock of Marblehead soon charged the fort, rounding up all the Southerners he could find. But upon taking inventory of the prisoners, he found that they were short eleven holdouts. All but one— Lanier, along with his bride, whose presence was as-yet unknown to the Yankees—surrendered.

In a frantic final tactic, Lanier feigned relinquishment, emerging from the excavated shaft with his hands raised. To Dimmock's surprise, he was followed by a quick-moving impish figure; she dashed out, putting her pistol to the neck of the nearest guard and demanded the colonel acquiesce and set them free.

Dimmock, although temporarily ruffled, moved toward her, offering calming words, attempting to disarm her. Perhaps believing she would be awarded reprieve, she let out a sigh—and Dimmock took his chance in the pacifying moment, attempting to knock her weapon from her hands. She fired, and the gun exploded, missing its target—instead sending a metal fragment into the brain of her husband standing nearby.

After all that time working to secure her beloved husband's freedom, it was she who dealt the blow that ultimately took him from her. Some accounts have her cradling him in her arms as he lost consciousness, passing out of this story and her life.

Two days later, Lanier was unceremoniously buried in an unmarked grave at the fort. Mrs. Lanier, for her part, no doubt in anguish, was declared a spy and ordered hanged.

And that moment is when she became the legend that pervades 150 years later. Just hours before her execution—perhaps in what she thought would be a staying tactic—she declared one final wish. Tired of concealing her gender in men's clothes, she said she wanted to wear a gown one final time before her death.

Certainly not an easy garment to come by at a military fort in the 1860s. Still, the men somehow came through, finding a garish black robe that might have once been worn by a stage actress, or even a monk. Last request granted, she was hanged, then interred beside her husband.

In a time when death and executions were simply an accepted part of day-to-day life, the fort soon got back to routine.

But it wasn't long before the strange occurrences began.

A few weeks later, as the lore goes, a young private was on night duty in the general vicinity of Mrs. Lanier's hanging spot. Suddenly, he felt a pair of hands clutch and squeeze his neck from behind. He whirled to see a woman dressed in black, face "contorted with rage," as recounted by Mascott Nadler. He was able to fend off the apparition but refused to return to his post and was punished with lock-up. The early 1890s was when the four soldiers came upon the unexplainable footprints in the snow; in another episode during World War II, a sentry devolved into an apoplectic fit and supposedly spent the ensuing decades in a psychiatric facility.

In other instances, her vengeful spirit was said to repeatedly tap shoulders from behind, answer phone calls, and endlessly roll a stone the length of a storeroom that was the traditional spot for a poker game—until the spooked men found another location for their revelry. She has also been heard warning, "Don't come in here!" to those attempting to approach the dungeon area, and soldiers have even shot at ghostlike apparitions chasing them. Other reports by those stationed at or visiting what is now a National Recreation Area have included lanterns held aloft by no hands, as well as an ethereal woman cloaked in a bonnet and shawl.

In some instances, her lore has been embraced with more playful frights. Before the fort was decommissioned in the 1940s, an officer had a wooden "tomb" set in the dirt in the "corridor of dungeons," according to *Mysterious New England*, compiled by Austin W. Stevens. When newcomers arrived, a girl or a soldier of shorter stature dressed in dark clothing would be hidden inside—and, after a storyteller finished recounting the legend of the mysterious Lady in

Black, would jump forth with a scream, terrifying unsuspecting listeners.

Ultimately, both the Laniers' remains were eventually removed from the fort. Where they lie—together or apart—remains unknown, fueling their mythos.

In the case of the Lady in Black, love indeed knows no bounds.

Or mercy.

Chapter 6

Castle Island:
Poe's Intrigue

Something wasn't right.

The layout of the historic fort's dungeon didn't match the blueprints. A full prisoner holding cell was missing. After a thorough inspection, the group of workmen, performing renovations to Boston Harbor's Fort Independence in 1905, determined why: One of the cells had been filled in from earthen floor to stone ceiling with layer upon layer of brick—although there had been no notation of the change in official records.

Pickaxes, sledgehammers, and trowels clanked against the makeshift edifice, pulling out chunks, cleaving through several layers of brick. Finally, the intrigued men had carved out a space large enough for one of their number to duck through into the mysteriously walled-in space.

Dingy with intermingling dirt and sweat, lantern held before him, the volunteer stepped through the craggy opening into the stiflingly dark cavity.

Tentative, fumbling steps, followed by a moment or two of silence.

Then an alarmed shout: There were human bones!

Imbued with curiosity and excitement, the men soon tore down the remainder of the enclosure, what they discovered to be an expedient tomb. Air and light that had been blocked out for decades revealed a ghastly find: a skeleton, the tattered remains of what looked like a mid-nineteenth-century military uniform draping its frame, ankles and wrists shackled in chains.

A body left to rot behind a false wall—it had a hauntingly familiar feel to it.

Nearly sixty years prior, in 1846, the godfather of the macabre, Edgar Allen Poe, first published one of his most legendary—and, particularly for the claustrophobic among us, decidedly sanity-splitting—short stories, "The Cask of Amontillado." Set in an unidentified Italian city, it is a nightmarish story of revenge in which Montresor, aggrieved for a number of personal infractions by his supposed friend, Fortunato, shackles the man up in a wine cellar amid the boisterous Lenten festival of Carnival. Tortuously laying down a wall of brick and mortar as his victim experiences the spectrum of emotions at his literally dead-ended predicament, Montresor then proceeds to seal the man in a living tomb.

Little could the working crew that happened upon the abandoned and unidentified skeleton within the catacombs of Fort Independence in the early twentieth century know that that notorious and distressing tale of retribution was purportedly inspired by a (then) little-known, lurid morsel of Boston lore (a touch of art imitating life, imitating art).

Initially constructed by the British in 1634 and located on Castle Island at the entrance of Boston's inner harbor, Fort Independence is one of the country's oldest fortified sites. The still-standing star-shaped fort was constructed prior to the Civil War, according to the Massachusetts Department of Conservation and Recreation, once the island was abandoned by the English after the American Revolution.

In May 1827, a newly enlisted soldier by the name of Edgar A. Perry arrived on-site; he would ultimately serve a five-month stay. Just eighteen years old and described as having brown hair and gray eyes, according to the research of local historian Edward Rowe Snow, the as-yet unknown would soon be recognized as the legendary Edgar Allan Poe.

Possessing the voracious curiosity characteristic of writers, he became fascinated with the grounds and history of the fort, often meandering it during patrols and off times. In one of his wanderings, he came upon a peculiar memorial engraved on all four sides: It was dedicated to twenty-one-year-old lieutenant Robert F. Massie, whose remains were deposited "beneath this stone," and who "fell near this spot" on December 25, 1817.

According to Rowe Snow, it was further inscribed: "The officers of the US Regiment of Lt. Art'y erected this monument as a testimony of their respect & friendship for an amiable man & Gallant officer."

Intrigued, Poe delved further, asking his fellow enlisted men what they had heard about the young soldier and his unfortunate death on Christmas Day just a decade earlier.

Eventually, he was able to patch together a story of a young life abbreviated by rash passion—and a horrifying method of revenge.

Jovial and friendly, Massie arrived at the fort in the year of his untimely death. Quick to make friends, the Virginia native was soon popular among his fellow men.

All but one—the only one that would ultimately count to history.

Capt. Gustavus Drane (referred to as "Green" in other circulating versions of the story) was quite the antagonist to Massie. Aggressive, caustic, and not at all favored among the men, he took an instant dislike to the young Virginian (perhaps out of jealousy because of the younger man's ease with his fellows; perhaps because polar opposites often breed contempt).

On the fateful Christmas Eve night in 1817, many of the fort's soldiers were obliged to stay on-duty. To pass the time—as they often did—they gathered for rounds of cards, both Drane and Massie included.

It didn't take long for the captain to became irked by the younger soldier's gaiety; soon enough, Drane threw down his cards and furiously accused Massie of cheating. A spar of words ensued and intensified, with both men refusing to acquiesce. The irate Drane finally challenged Massie to a duel the following morning to satiate his honor. Despite the entreaties of his friends—largely due to the fact that his commanding officer was far more advanced with a sword—the younger man stubbornly agreed.

The following morning, Christmas Day, the fort awoke early, abuzz with anticipation. The two adversaries met outside the barracks, the duel commencing as the dull winter sun began its daily crescendo across the sky.

Fate was rapidly decided. A superior and much more experienced fighter, Drane fatally stabbed Massie in the chest. As he gloated in his victory, the soldiers carried Massie inside, keeping him as comfortable as possible until his death later that day.

Both saddened and enraged by the loss of their friend—and also as a means of outright protest—the men at the fort quickly erected a prominent memorial and ceremoniously buried Massie.

And soon, after learning that this was a sociopathic pattern of Drane's—he had supposedly been involved in the killings of up to six other soldiers in duels—they conspired a revenge.

One night not long after Massie's murder, several of the men gathered with the captain; acting especially friendly and subservient, they baited him with copious amounts of wine. Soon drunk beyond his senses, Drane was deadloaded by the men into the dark and dusky chambers below the fort, which housed its disused dungeon. Before his inebriated mind could grasp what was happening, Drane's hands and legs were shackled in iron cuffs in one of the small cells, and the men were making rapid work of trapping him in with rows of stone and grout.

Much like his fictional likeness Fortunato, the captain quickly sobered, fermenting with rage and demanding to be released. Ignoring his barked appeals that quickly devolved to blubbering pleas, methodical in their reprisal, the men kept at it. Finally, they sealed up the hastily—but sturdily built—wall with a final brick, reducing Drane's hoarse and weakening yelps to suffocating echoes.

Following the deed, to avoid interrogation or conviction, many of the men supposedly requested leave; some deserted; others, perhaps afflicted by a guilty conscience, claimed to see a Drane's phantom floating idly around the barracks. Such sporadic reports of a ghostly form persist to this day.

All told, it was a fantastical story; particularly for a morbidly creative mind such as Poe, who recorded all the details that he could on the skirmish and the live burial that followed.

His fellow soldiers, though, unsettled by the burgeoning writer's obsession with the gruesome tale, reported him to superior officers. They called him in, questioned him, assured him that it was just an urban legend, then asked him to promise not to spread the outlandish tale.

Poe agreed, never speaking of the story—until publishing the eerily similar "Amontillado" nearly twenty years later.

When Drane's ragged remains were supposedly discovered in the depths of the fort, there was no way to identify them (which leads some to believe that it truly is nothing more than the product of an imaginative mind—Poe's or otherwise). It's said the skeleton was given a full military funeral, then buried in a grave marked UNKNOWN in Fort Independence's cemetery.

The young Massie, for his part, also experienced an unsettled afterlife (although it wasn't nearly as ghastly as his attacker's). For reasons that aren't entirely clear, his body was dug up and reburied three times in a matter of 122 years—it was first relocated from Castle Island to the nearby Governor's Island, then again to Deer Island, then finally (we can assume) to Fort Devens, west of the city. As a result of his posthumous travels, Massie became known as the "Roving Skeleton of Boston Bay."

But the fallout of the infamous duel isn't the island's only presumed history of the supernatural.

According to Rowe Snow, some have long declared the enclave as cursed. Prior to the American Revolution, as legend goes, an Englishman living on the isle desired for his beautiful daughter to marry a British officer. She, however, had already declared her love for an American boy. The two suitors fought for her, and the British soldier was victorious. Heartbroken, the girl took her own life. Shattered in turn, her spurned, would-be husband plunged into the ocean, declaring as he drowned that his specter would curse anyone who came near the island.

Some believe that the ensuing shipwrecks not far offshore, as well as an inordinate number of murders, suicides, and drownings on or near the island, are the result of his bitter dying words.

Poe, for his part, moved on from Fort Independence and from Boston—which in time he grew to despise. He once famously said that "their pumpkin pies are delicious. Their poetry is not so good," and used the pejorative "Frogpondians" to refer to its celebrated transcendentalist authors, such as Henry David Thoreau, as Nicholas Goodwin describes in *Spooky Creepy Boston*.

He also declared that the city's dwellers had "no soul" and were "well bred—as very dull persons generally are."

But Boston ultimately gets the final word on the matter; a city so "dull" could never inspire such a macabre, disturbing tale of revenge.

Chapter 7
Nixes Mate

Since time immemorial, civilizations—Boston included—have concocted ingeniously grotesque methods to create spectacles of their miscreants. Crucifixion, impaling, stoning, burning, hanging, tarring and feathering, displaying heads on pikes—all have served as shocking practices to both punish and deter.

According to Boston historian Edward Rowe Snow, some torturous and humiliating methods that were either invented or borrowed for tradition's sake in the city during the seventeenth and eighteenth centuries included branding, maiming, slicing off ears, slitting nostrils, and boring tongues through with hot irons. The presumed guilty were also assigned letters of guilt akin to Nathaniel Hawthorne's adulteress Hester Prynne—for example, *B* for blasphemy, *D* for drunkenness, or *V* for pure viciousness—constrained from speaking, eating and drinking with a scold's bridle (essentially a metal human muzzle), and threatened with drowning on a ducking stool, a chair attached to a seesaw apparatus that immersed them in water for whatever length of time their tormenters saw fit (used especially to cure "scolding women" and "chyderers," according to Rowe Snow).

When it came to pirates riding in on the tide of the roiling Atlantic, meanwhile, the favored method was a gibbet. Essentially a body-conforming cage, it was used to dangle corpses at the harbor's entrance to serve as an omen and a warning to others who might be plotting plunder or outright mayhem. Gruesomely, the contraption was very often left to hang for months or even years, as the bodies inside rotted, festered and withered; bones, hair and garments slowly bleached out by the searing sun and deteriorated by the insistent gnawing of salt, sand, and time.

Nixes Mate, one of Boston Harbor's smallest islands, was once a prominent site for such loathsome displays. The islet itself is said to be named for—and purportedly also cursed by—one particularly wronged pirate.

Difficult as it is to fathom that exotic, dangerous, swashbuckling, treasure-hunting outlaws once trolled the Puritanical New England coast, a form of pirating was actually sanctioned by the Massachusetts state legislature as the American Revolution began to rage in 1775; privateers were given unrestricted authority to harass, plunder, and take prisoners from merchant ships.

The story of Nixes Mate begins, as is fitting, out on the open sea. Captain Nix, fitting the cliché of a cruel and merciless ship commander quick to dole out punishment, was abhorred by his crew. Finally fed up, his men mutinied, and under ambiguous circumstances, he was murdered, his body inevitably consumed by the sea.

The crew was soon marshaled back to dry land, taken into custody, and interrogated. Each and every man, when questioned in his turn, blamed the fiasco on the first mate (Nix's mate, whose given or chosen names did not withstand the corrosive quality of time).

On tenuous charges, the man was quickly tried, convicted, and sentenced. Although he staunchly maintained his innocence, he was shipped out for execution to what was soon to become his namesake island. As the noose was cinched and ready, he offered his final ominous words: Because he was being wrongfully put to death, the "ghastly isle" would be destroyed, according to Joseph A. Citro's *Cursed in New England: Stories of Damned Yankees.* "Mark my words, for they will ensure that no such abomination of justice can ever occur here again," he was said to have prophesied before the hangman performed his somber duty.

And over time—whether by curse or coincidence—his revelation has proved true. The tiny island, identified today by a square granite buttress and an octagonal beacon, has been voraciously consumed by the sea. At certain times, depending on the tide, it is diminished to a mere sliver cresting above water—certainly not, as the doomed mate foretold centuries ago, large enough to support a gallows.

Even so, its size belies its history; yet another pirate legend pervades Nixes Mate.

William Fly was a well-known—and widely feared— marauder who had an intensely brief but prolific, barbarous pirating career off the New England coast. In 1726, he started out as a boatswain on a ship traveling from Jamaica to West Africa. Quickly, though, he advanced his station by sparking a revolt, taking over the ship and renaming it the foreboding *Fame's Revenge*, then turning it toward the American coast. Throughout his short but bloody campaign, during which he was said to dole out copious and excessively severe lashings, he and his crew were successful in capturing a half-dozen other ships—before being caught themselves by authorities off the Newburyport coast. The callous Fly was then taken to Boston, tried, rapidly convicted, and sentenced to hang on Nixes Mate.

And a final moment of fearless defiance secured his notoriety for the ages.

Noticing that his hangman was an amateur who fumbled with knots, Fly purportedly yanked the rope from the astonished man's hands, tied a noose, then slung it around his own neck. After his execution, he was left to hang as a premonitory tactic, before being eventually buried on the island alongside two fellow outlaws.

Still, although piracy has long since waned along with the tide—on the North American coast, at least—its specters are said to continue with their terrorizing ways, leering and taunting. Various ships passing by Nixes Mate over the years have reported mysterious lights with no origin, creepy laughs, jeers, whispers, and even agonized screams.

Elsewhere up and down the Massachusetts seacoast, pirate legacies are said to endure through the continued discovery of their most cherished (albeit usurped) possessions. Numerous diamonds, pearls, jewelry, and coins of varied origin have been dug up and unearthed by pure luck, found lodged in chests or scattered along the Boston seashore and local river beds—representing untold amounts that may still be concealed in the depths beneath.

Chapter 8

Lighting the Way to Tragedy

Lighthouses have long been romanticized as sentinels of the sea—watchtowers, guideposts, witnesses to catastrophe, fortune, heartbreak, and touching reunions. Boston Head Light, the country's oldest-standing (and second-oldest working) beacon has been a silent observer to the panorama of human emotion and experience—spectral and otherwise.

As is the case with many structures that have stood for centuries, the three-hundred-year-old guiding light has also been a bystander to, and a participant in, an inordinate amount of tragedy.

Calamity struck almost immediately after its inaugural lighting in September 1716. Located on Little Brewster Island in the outer harbor, its first caretaker was George Worthylake, who settled on the enclave with his wife and two daughters. Not two years later, after several months of faithfully tending the light, he, his wife, one of his daughters (as well as an unknown passenger, it was said) drowned when the boat they were rowing capsized on a return trip from Boston.

Ensuing keepers of the white conical tower overlooking the Atlantic had no simpler go of it; watching helplessly as the ocean dashed ships against its granite ledge or suffering drowning deaths themselves, they were also continually bombarded by decimating storms, icy gales, consuming tides, fires, lightning strikes, and assaults of the British during the Revolutionary War.

One of the most famous wrecks was of the rigger *Maritana* in 1861; a winter squall smashed it into the barren "shag rocks" northeast of Brewster Island, destroying the vessel and washing debris ashore for months.

In an eerie tale recounted by Patricia Hughes in the book *More Lost Loot*, twenty years following its devastation, a middle-aged couple named Chardon rented out a room at the lighthouse. The wife had lost her memory years before but was curiously drawn to Boston Light, and the anticipation was that her visit there might jostle a remembrance or recollection.

As it turns out, it did—but not nearly as her loved ones had hoped.

While the couple was there, Englishman Edward Moraine, one of the few *Maritana* survivors, visited to reflect on the calamity. Upon seeing him, the woman screamed and sobbed inconsolably. Her memory had indeed returned—she recalled that her name was Alice, and she recognized the man as her first husband. As he reached for her, she recoiled and disappeared into the dark. Shortly thereafter, her body was found on Shag Rocks (where it was believed her restless spirit had actually perished twenty-two years earlier with her fellow *Maritana* passengers).

Meanwhile, over the years, keepers have reported shadows and footsteps without human origin throughout the tower and its lantern room, as well as the purported ghost of an old sailor who deviously fiddles with radios whenever rock and roll comes on.

A "ghost walk" seven miles east of the beacon is also said to be something of an enigma. Its atmosphere is not penetrated by sound—it is devoid of voices, waves, and Head Light's wide-reaching warning bell. The phenomenon has been so confounding that a group of students from the Massachusetts Institute of Technology were said to spend a summer there investigating it—but much like the numerous other wonders suspended within the churning, rolling depths of the Boston Harbor, it remains a mystery.

Part 4

GRAVE MATTERS

Take a step or two closer. Lean in. Squinch your eyes to make out the engravings on the centuries-old stones effaced and worn by time and the elements.

Drab or elaborate, succinct or wordy, poetic or prosaically and emotionlessly listing names and dates, they represent passing eras and shifting sentiments, identifying the remains—both physical and, in some cases it's said, spectral—of the many who came before. Luminaries and legends who triumphed and lost, founding fathers and mothers, revolutionaries, scapegoats, martyrs, enemies, lovers, unknowns, and common, everyday men and women.

Boston and its environs are location to many of the country's oldest and most historic burial grounds, a ghastly gratifying sentiment for coimetromaniacs (a term to describe those who are naturally—or unnaturally—lured to cemeteries). Step through their gates, walk their trodden paths, and listen to—and maybe even walk with—the dead who dwell within.

Chapter 9

A Walk through Old North Church's Underground Crypts

Descend three stone steps to an entry set into a brick edifice, pass through a pale red wooden door. Enter a narrow, serene, mutely lit columbarium adorned with crosses and candles, walls inlaid with slate square niches containing cremated ashes. Walk to a slim passage jaggedly cut into stone; step over the threshold and down, duck your head.

There, you find yourself standing among the dead in a once-neglected, centuries-old crypt.

The confined, dusky, low-ceilinged recess—outer walls and inner chamber made of brick, once-earthen floor now layered with concrete—is just below the sanctuary of Boston's revered and historic Old North Church. Mere feet above your head, the wooden floor of the city's longest-surviving chapel protests with a litany of grunts and grumbles under the weight of its constant ebb of visitors.

All told, there are thirty-seven tombs carved into this catacomb where shadow dominates over light. They are estimated to hold 1,100 souls, entombed between the 1730s and the 1850s. But as you tour the dim corridors, dipping your head under pipes, peering around dark bends, shuffling past detritus from the church's nearly three-hundred-year history, you see that they are not among the many historymakers, notables, or even notorious who rest below the depths of this venerable city. Interred in arched vaults and bricked up for the unknown great beyond, these are the everyday Bostonians. Those who crowded its early cobblestone streets, purchased its goods, celebrated and worshiped in its taverns and churches, gathered with relatives and friends in its early homes—ultimately living the history that defined this country, witnessing it unfold.

Still, for years, they were truly abandoned to time.

Built in 1723, Old North Church has been revered for its role in the first days of the American Revolution as a crucial signaling post—via two lanterns hung just briefly on its steeple—that British troops were marching on Lexington and Concord. For years, though, as that significant moment in American history was touted above, the hundreds of dead dwelling below were abandoned in their dank and dusty eternal resting chambers.

The church adopted the practice, imported from their European ancestors, as a space-saving tactic—and, no less notably, as a means to raise funds. The first burials occurred in 1732, and the privilege was at first reserved for Old North's wealthiest families who could afford the luxury—but that was eventually broadened out to include almost anyone (even the North End neighborhood's most deplorable residents—including those without physical addresses to call their own). The tradition continued until the 1850s, when city officials outlawed underground burials (although the church, defiant of the order, didn't immediately cease the practice). Once the crypt was finally sealed, however, it was summarily forgotten, particularly as the country became consumed in the Civil War and the immense impacts of its outcome.

But then, a few years ago, Jane Lynden Rousseau, a funerary archaeologist from Harvard's Peabody Museum, set to researching the bowels of the church; it was reopened for study for the first time in centuries, and, eventually, for regular guided tours. "This basement is bursting with bones," Lynden Rousseau told ABC News in April 2009.

Quite literally. Based on her research, as original wooden doors rotted and decayed, body parts spilled into the antechamber. They were then heaved back in and the entry resealed with more wood reinforced by wire and concrete.

Smaller chambers were set into the brick walls of the perimeter, larger ones into a center enclosure. The bigger ones could hold—no doubt rather snugly—up to forty spartan coffins that were cut down to as little material as possible, essentially formfitting to bodies buried in stockings or white robes. A small window in the casket lid allowed mourners one last view of the dead; it was boarded up when the bodies were interred.

Over time, it didn't take long for the already cramped space to fill up. As the parish grew along with the city, the bodies of strangers were unceremoniously added to family tombs. Continued limited availability spurred an even more gruesome practice: Workers would unseal the oldest tombs and simply sweep them out, clearing them of deteriorated bones, scraps of burial clothing, clumps of hair, as well as decades upon decades of accumulated dirt and dust. If they could, they would leave the skulls and collarbones of their original inhabitants—for posterity or perhaps out of a sense of superstition or obligated reverence for the dead. The remainder would then be dumped inelegantly into what's known as a charnel pit, dating to medieval times, essentially a repository for the hodgepodge of assorted bones unearthed during grave digging.

As you glance around the dark, simply lit space, pervasive with the mingling balm of mildew and dust common to areas occupied by the dead, you can feel a sense of unease, of claustrophobia, of confinement. Around you, set into the mottled and blanched brick walls, are tombs both anonymous and prominently marked.

Here lies Samuel Nicholson, first commander of the USS *Constitution*, memorialized with a contemporary gold plaque bearing gold lettering (that is still, as noted by your tour guide, to this day frequented by current and former members of the naval forces). Over there is Ann Ruggles, identified with the sparse "Tomb 1742" etched into a rectangle of slate. Nearby are Bostones Shubael Bell and Robert Fennelly, buried in 1808 and commemorated with the iconic arched gravestone slab (set into the wall) common to early American cemeteries.

There is also the church's first minister, Timothy Cutler, whose sleep was disturbed to ensure his eternal presence here. Originally buried elsewhere, he was exhumed and reinterred in the tomb of a wealthy family who deigned to hold the distinction of lying beside their beloved church's first reverend.

Elsewhere, time has etched away at once-crisp lettering, making some stones set square into the walls frustratingly illegible; other openings are closed, forever impersonal to the ages, by large rectangular slabs of concrete.

Others are purposely nameless; as you round a shadowy passage, you come upon a marker inscribed, "No. 14 / Stranger's Tomb / 1813." It was here that the derelict and destitute were buried out of necessity or as an act of spiritual charity. At the outbreak of a smallpox epidemic during the War of 1812, as many victims who succumbed to the virus as could be were wedged into the space, literally stacked floor to ceiling, and the chamber was immediately closed to prevent the spread of disease.

It's believed that one hundred or so redcoats also lie here in anonymity, as well as one British Marine officer who was the victim of posthumous mistaken identity. When the family of Maj. John Pitcairn, who led antagonist forces in Lexington and Concord and was later felled at the Battle of Bunker Hill, came to retrieve his body, they were not able to positively distinguish him. So, it was said, they chose the corpse clad in the highest-ranking uniform. As legend goes, in his stead, they returned to England and unknowingly buried the body of a Lieutenant Shea.

As you navigate the warren-like underground alleys— the constant groans and creaks from above serving as a sort of artificial thunder that threatens to rend the ceiling open—you pass by the variety of dead telling their tales (or, conversely, keeping them hushed for all time), as well as the sentimental sediment of the passing ages. You edge past stacks of bricks awaiting a purpose and antique bell wheels from the 191-foot-high steeple above; step around lecterns coated with years' worth of dust, boilers, boxes, sections of fencing, and filing cabinets; dodge water pipes snaking through the dusk overhead.

The dead lying just feet from you in their beds of brick might follow your progress, wary of the curious-looking visitors in their midst; or, content to have been discovered once again, they may simply lie at peace in their slumber.

In either case, as you step back out into the modern sepulchral vault, you're likely to cast a glance back, cognizant of the crucial importance of the so-called unimportant who lie within. Everyday men and women, those whose names are only recalled by their loved ones or on their epitaphs—not recorded in history or in books or on plaques—but who ultimately, collectively, served as the shaping and shifting evolutionary force of early America.

Chapter 10
Copp's Hill Burying Ground

Climb a steep hill directly across from the entry to Old North Church—passing by tourists seeking that oh-so-perfect shot of the renowned, 191-foot steeple, fighting limited angles on a cramped, sharply inclined street obscured by encroaching brownstones—to a burial ground set several feet above the sidewalk. Ivy drapes down along its brick buttress; up a few precipitous steps, stone walkways meander among hundreds of markers, an encircling wrought-iron fence hemming in the spirits here.

Established in 1659, Copp's Hill is the city's second-oldest funerary ground—and it is storied with a history of dead both disturbed and restless. Although the estimates seem inconceivable given its mere visual size, it is believed that between 10,000 and 11,000 interments took place within its limits over more than three centuries.

Named for the shoemaker William Copp who once owned it, it was bought up in four different parcels over two hundred years, as the growing city's dead threatened to overflow the realm of the living (but history, as often turns out, would prove quite the reverse).

Among the notables sleeping—comfortably or not—within its depths are influential father-and-son Puritan ministers Increase Mather and Cotton Mather (who would both come to be most-remembered and admonished for their roles in the hysterics in Salem—the father, Increase, for his tepid pleas of moderation; the son, Cotton, for his rabid support); first Boston Light keeper George Worthylake, who died tragically on duty (and, in a perhaps morbid touch of irony, his headstone, shared with his wife and daughter and featuring winged skull iconography, is pitched slightly and half-sunken into the ground); and Old North Church sexton Robert Newman, who placed the signal lanterns atop the steeple and secured his place in history. More than 1,000 African Americans from a free community started in 1650 and known as "New Guinea" are also thought to be buried at Copp's Hill (many in unmarked graves, or what might have once been wooden graves that rotted away with the centuries). That includes one-time slave Prince Hall of Medford, who was believed to fight in the Revolutionary War, was a noted abolitionist and advocate for the education of black children, and founded the first Masonic Lodge for African Americans.

Still, in a young, growing country where desperation can be a symptom of turbulent times and circumstance, it wasn't long before the dead were agitated in their repose.

Grave diggers were some of the first to raise the lifeless bodies; exhumed coffins were reported to be haphazardly heaped and stacked along with the decaying parts of those who once lay inside them. Cracked apart, the caskets revealed bits of clothing, as well as clinging skin and hair. Mother Nature did her work, as well—during especially heavy rains, so much dirt was washed away in runnels leading down the hill to the Charles River that the lids of coffins became exposed.

Meanwhile, some of the oldest stones were desecrated by vandals—or altered brashly by those who simply felt entitled to a place of rest, whether or not it was already taken.

Church sexton Samuel Winslow was said to have merchant William Clark's name etched away and replaced with his own on a tomb unique to the colonial era featuring cornucopias of fruit and an elaborate coat of arms with a knight's head plate. Similarly, the grave of city forefather Thomas Hutchinson and his family was co-opted by Thomas Lewis; it's not known for sure who ultimately lies beneath.

"Their bones are now scattered before the four winds of heaven!" Thomas Bridgman exclaimed in his 1851 catalog of Copp's Hill epitaphs. "Their tomb has passed into the hands of strangers."

Other markers were yanked out of the ground and used as planks or platforms for their neighbors by grave diggers performing their duties. Still others were employed for more mundane—but no less disturbing—purposes. When tenement houses began to emerge around the burial ground, headstones were removed and used to cover drains or chimneys and replace roof tiles; were incorporated into house foundations, cellars, and road improvement projects; and, in one completely grotesque practice, according to author Christopher Forest, one cook put one to use as a baking plate. Showing further disrespect for the dead, tenants would run their laundry over and through the cemetery, and allow their cats to pass unheeded throughout its limits.

Eternal sleep was also interrupted by British soldiers, who mounted cannons atop the hill. They were also said to be particularly ruthless with the stone of oenophile Daniel Malcolm, a member of the Sons of Liberty who smuggled dozens of casks of wine into Boston. Topped with a classic eighteenth-century skull-and-crossbones icon, the grave of the forty-four-year-old who was a "Friend to the Publick and Enemy to oppression," as carved on his epitaph, is clearly pockmarked with at least four holes that were said to be caused by English soldiers honing their musketry.

Perhaps for these various infringements over the centuries, Copp's Hill has been known for its supernatural occurrences. Visitors, from the unsuspecting to paranormal researchers, have reported several unexplained forms, shadows cast by no discernible beings, as well as numerous orbs, from streaks, blurs, or veritable flurries of them. Some have even said to have seen the apparitions of little girls flitting among the tombstones, as well as women dressed in flowing period garb.

Maybe further expressing displeasure at their discomposure, there have been at least two significant (and tragic) events nearby. One was the so-called Molasses Flood of 1919, in which a tank of the thick, dark brown syrup exploded, according to The Bostonian Society, overtaking railroad tracks and buildings in a forty-foot wave and killing twenty-one people. Another was the 1950 Brinks robbery, the then-largest bank heist in the United States that was deemed "the crime of the century." Roughly a dozen men in Halloween masks absconded with roughly $2.7 million in cash, checks, money orders, and other securities, according to the Federal Bureau of Investigation (all were later caught, tried, and convicted, although only a fraction of the loot was ultimately recovered).

Today, though, the historical necropolis is mostly a site of calm (albeit for those drifting spirits who occasionally make themselves known). Brick walkways and paths where grass has ceded its perennial effort to dirt weave among the markers. Some, apparently without a final home, line the gated perimeter, bearing a variety of dates and names, appearing in numerous states of damage and decay. The others, mostly classic slate, are lined up in neat rows frequented by tweeting and fluttering sparrows; some are lichen covered, others cleaved, a few expunged of their inscriptions. Still others lean against each other, as if seeking comfort and solace against the loneliness of death.

Chapter 11

King's Chapel Burying Ground

As the legend goes, arrive under the cask of night. Cross into the cemetery gates. Choose a stone (any stone); rap on it three times. Then inquire of the dark, "Captain Kidd, for what were you hanged?"

So it's said, you may feel a sudden, distinctive presence; someone skulking close, watching. But if you ask again, the infamous pirate, enduringly defiant in his innocence, will not answer.

To most, this is a bogus urban legend perpetuated by youth and coy tour guides. (Disclaimer: Don't actually try it; all city cemeteries close at 5 p.m.—so the biggest scare you're likely to get is from a cool set of handcuffs.)

But it is the sort of story that permeates Boston's oldest graveyard—and what is said to be its most haunted, where everlasting inhabitants have encountered the worst kinds of luck.

Located adjacent to—but not affiliated with—King's Chapel (built in 1686, fifty years after the graveyard was laid out, and now a Unitarian Universalist church), the cemetery was established in 1630 on what was then the outskirts of the new Puritan settlement. An estimated 1,000 people are buried within, the earliest of them English-born settlers who ventured to the New World in pursuit of what they believed would be a better, freer life. Again literally pressed by constrained space in a burgeoning capital city, officials ultimately overcrowded it, continuing burials until around 1896.

Roughly six hundred stones and twenty-nine tabletop tombs identify its occupants; as Christopher Forest explains in *Boston's Haunted History*, graves could contain as many as twenty people, with just one headstone as a reminder of the final one in.

Among those who forever seek repose here: John Winthrop (the elder), founder of Boston and first (and twelve-term) governor of the Massachusetts Bay Colony; Mary (Chilton) Winslow, believed to be the first European woman to disembark the *Mayflower*; William Dawes, a man of many trades who literally went along for Paul Revere's famous ride; Francis Brinley, the wealthiest man in eighteenth-century Boston; Frederic Tudor, who established the Tudor Ice Company and effectively became known as the "Ice King"; as well as several progressive, so-called she-merchants who were both successful and well respected by their male counterparts.

But other lesser-knowns intrigue, as well.

For example: A stubby stone, slightly askance, subtly weathered, with a hunk of its right finial missing, sits on the right edge of the grounds. Along with more classic iconography such as a skull with wings, it bears a striped coat of arms with the letter *A* accompanied by two lions. Its engraving reads, "Here Lyes Ye Body of Elizabeth Pain Wife to Samuel Pain / Aged near 52 years / Departed this life November 26, 1704." According to historian Robert Shackleton, Pain was an old maid who, out of wedlock, bore a child who died at a young (unknown) age. She was brought to trial for murder, but although acquitted, was found guilty of negligence, for which she was fined and publicly flogged. While many contend that the *A* is simply a family crest, some have speculated that Nathaniel Hawthorne, in his walks around the city, saw the tombstone, and was inspired to write one of his greatest works, *The Scarlet Letter*. (Although the author himself recalled how he was prompted by a worn *A* he discovered in an attic.)

Meanwhile, one of the burial site's most ornamented stones is a remembrance to twenty-three-year-old shopkeeper Joseph Tapping, who died in 1678. Believed to be the work of the famed unknown "Charlestown Stonecutter," if features Latin inscriptions and an hourglass atop a winged skull, and bears an intricate relief of Father Time (represented as a bearded figure with wings) attempting to halt a skeleton (signifying death) from snuffing out the flame of life.

But it's said that many of the dead here are truly lost souls—awoken from their slumber by various intrusions, their afterlife disquieted and disoriented.

It didn't take long for meddlers to intrude. In 1686, Edmund Andros, who was appointed governor of New England by King James II, built King's Chapel, unapologetically displacing several of the dead buried in a corner of the cemetery. Further displacement occurred in later years when the church was rebuilt and expanded, as well as when the subway ventilation shaft was installed (a round structure topped off and hemmed in by a grate, and appearing like a giant bottomless well near the entrance of the burial ground, it serves as an unmarked curiosity to visitors).

But what some consider the most egregious disturbance took place in 1810. By the turn of the 19th century, as the city was undergoing rapid growth and development, and the graveyard was becoming unkempt; corners of caskets and even body parts were said to occasionally emerge from the soil like gruesome growths. The superintendent of burials, with what can be assumed as good intentions, pulled out the existing headstones and rearranged them in orderly rows—neglecting, in the process, where each marker had originally been set.

His carelessness drew ire and dismay. Boston lawyer and historian Nathaniel Ingersoll Bowditch, in a column in the newspaper *The Gleaner*, called himself a witness to the "truly sacrilegious act." "The result," he wrote, "is that the tear of affection may hereafter be shed; or the sigh of sentiment breathed, in a wrong locality, and perhaps the bones of a stranger instead of an ancestor, may be piously gathered and entombed anew by a descendant, unsuspecting of so strange and inexcusable an outrage."

The ultimate disrespect is said to have caused endless confusion. Spirits, lost and unsure of the location of their final resting places, are believed to roam the cemetery, robbed of their timeless sleep.

But King's Chapel is host to even more unsettling stories. In 1820, for instance, an old man was rumored to be buried alive by his family members seeking to get at his wealth. At the insistence of an old woman who was sure that he lay underground still mortal, a mob developed, and to appease them, the man was exhumed (and found dead). Whether be was interred devoid of vitality, or indeed buried alive and suffered to perish in one of the most ghastly ways possible, is only known to him (or his alleged tormentors). In another tale of horror and desecration, a woman was being prepared for interment when her hapless casket maker realized his (literally) grave mistake: Her coffin was too short. So, it was said, embarrassed and not wanting to expose the mishap, he sawed off her head, wedged it between her legs, then nailed the lid shut. Some believe the nameless (and headless) woman endlessly seeks to avenge the indignity, aimlessly drifting throughout the burial ground.

Then there are the legends of Capt. William Kidd, whose famed treasure is still sought to this day. (In 2015, for example, underwater archaeologists pulled a 110-pound silver bar out of the shallow depths of the waters off Madagascar that they identified as belonging to the infamous British pirate.) As the lore goes, his disgraced bones were secretly buried in an unmarked mound within King's Chapel Burying Ground (although the general belief is that his remains lie somewhere, no doubt unidentified, in his native England).

Kidd, a sailor, was supposedly sent out in the 1690s as a privateer to pursue pirates—and then purportedly became one. (His guilt in this area is heavily contested by historians.) He was arrested in Boston in 1701 and summarily shipped to England, where he was adamant in his probity. Nonetheless, he was hanged, his dead body left dangling in a gibbet, as was the custom, to literally keep other pirates at bay.

Still, some profess to feel his ruthless presence trolling King's Chapel's confined grounds. And in addition to the urban legend that his ghost can be raised with a few knocks and a simple question, visitors have also claimed malfunctions in their cameras and recording devices—batteries draining, inability to call up video footage—that miraculously go away once they step out of the cemetery gates onto the sidewalk.

In any case, though, King's Chapel is indeed a treasure trove.

Chapter 12

Granary Burying Ground

Located just steps from the Boston Common and the Massachusetts State House, the Granary Burying Ground is where Massachusetts' most eminent hold their final gathering. The third-oldest cemetery in Boston, established in 1660 and named for a 12,000-bushel grain warehouse that once stood close by, it serves as the final bed for some of the city's—and, ultimately, the country's—most significant influencers.

Paul Revere, John Hancock, Robert Treat Paine, and Samuel Adams are all buried here, along with five patriots killed in the Boston Massacre, and twelve-year-old Christopher Snyder, whose fatal shot to the stomach by a Tory sympathizer precipitated the event in March 1770. There are also various mayors, governors and Sons of Liberty here, as well as purveyors of legend such as Mary Balston Vergoose—believed to be the inspiration for the legendary Mother Goose—who purportedly passed on her gift of storytelling to her "gaggle" of ten children.

Estimates put the number of dead within Granary's sprawling expanse at 8,000, although only just about a quarter of those are identified—the cemetery has 2,345 gravestones and 204 tombs.

Its vast array of souls seems to have emboldened at least a few resident specters. There have been reports of a roving apparition dressed in colonial garb, and due to a high amount of recorded phenomena, paranormal researchers consider the ground among the city's most haunted. Numerous visitors—believers and not—have claimed to have captured ethereal noises, shady figures, and various floating objects with their phones and cameras (sights and sounds they weren't witness to in person). Beyond its large number of occupants, another reason for roving entities could be a common practice that was undertaken as centuries, boundaries, and sentiments shifted. As was the case at King's Chapel Burying Ground, markers here have been hauled out of the ground and "tidied" into clean lines on at least two occasions—perhaps causing infinite disorientation on the part of the dead.

But also given that it is one of the larger cemeteries in Boston proper, its stones feature an array of iconography reflecting shifting sentiments on the afterlife. Those include the post-Revolutionary weeping willow and urn, hourglasses, skeletons, robed figures holding sickles, and multiple variations on the winged skull, winged cherub, and skull-and-crossbones symbols that represent life, death, and fleeting time. Other unique stones within feature lengthy Latin carvings in impeccable calligraphy, and tabletop graves—slabs laid flat on four legs—bear what appear to be offerings in the way of clusters of pennies.

So ultimately, the 355-year-old burial ground is architecturally—as well as spectrally and historically—intriguing.

Chapter 13

Exclusive Places of Rest

Just as in life, the dead express themselves in a variety of ways—the Boston area is replete with tombs and markers that are blazingly unique, utterly perplexing, and exceptionally creepy.

SINISTER SENTINEL

Arms outstretched, head upturned, her face is stern and resolute, black-hollowed eyes cold and pitiless. Spreading wide a giant cloak to reveal her matronly form draped in a revealing dress, it seems that at any moment she could descend from her pedestal to enshroud unsuspecting victims in her mantle, suffocating them in a black, dead embrace.

She is Witch Bonney, a patinaed bronze statue that keeps formidable watch over Lowell Cemetery, a pastoral burial ground in its namesake mill city west of Boston known for its historic role in the Industrial Revolution. Guarding the entrance to the nineteenth-century Bonney family tomb, the supposed sorceress is both eerie and entrancing, terrifying and ghastly in her decay—a sooty silhouette of incrustation threatens to eventually consume her in darkness, tracing her facial features, neck, arms, and bare shoulders; clinging to her dress and the inside of her immense shawl.

As legend has it, she is cursed by the spirit of an enchantress who was assassinated when her gifts were discovered—and in a peculiarly provocative way. The effigy's barely-there frock threatens to slip from her shoulders and expose her breasts; it is said that each year her décolletage falls lower and lower, and that once it finally succumbs to gravity, dropping to her waist and fully baring her chest, the witch will awaken to finally enact her acrimony pent up by centuries.

It's unclear where or how the story originated—little is known about the Bonney family, particularly whether they were involved in witchcraft—but the superstitious nonetheless yield to it, purportedly pacifying her vindictive spirit by leaving tokens and offerings such as coins and flowers at her bare bronze feet.

But whether or not she does get her reprisal, it's said that Witch Bonney, in turn, has an abiding guard—her protector or her keeper? Only the dead here know.

The eighty-five-acre burial ground, dedicated in 1814, is also the location of perpetual quietude for a life-sized white lion. Maned and majestic, resting on a pedestal, it was commissioned in 1888 for the grave of nineteenth-century millionaire James Cook Ayer, a manufacturer of medicinal products who spent his final days in an asylum and died in 1878. His tomb was carved by celebrated London sculptor Price Joy and is considered such an investment that it is protected every winter with a customized wooden structure. Making it remarkable is both its realism and its size: Eight feet high, twelve feet long, it weighs around twenty-five tons (the combined weight of a pride of it and its brethren—several times over).

So ultimately, you could call Lowell Cemetery a tale of the lion, the witch and . . . the disappearing wardrobe?

MONUMENT TO THE MACABRE

As the inimitably bizarre Edgar Allen Poe affirmed, there is no circumstance in the world more "unquestioningly poetical" than the death of a beautiful woman. The vulgar, horrific murder of Elizabeth "Betty" Short—obscure in her life and infamous in her death, when she was immediately branded with the nickname "the Black Dahlia"—has inspired many lamentations, fictionalizations, and analyses (poetic and not) throughout popular culture. Nearly seventy years later, her vile slaying remains among the oldest cold-case files in the history of Los Angeles.

And although she was ultimately buried in Oakland, California, identified with a simple stone marker that makes no mention of the dreadful nickname that relentlessly pursued her in death, the story of her sensational, heinous murder is immortalized with an unexpected (and rather unassuming, for the casual passerby) plaque in her hometown just outside Boston.

Born in the Hub and raised in its suburb of Medford, twenty-two-year-old Short was an aspiring actress who relocated to Hollywood. Like many who emigrate to that burg of broken dreams, she covered her bills with a waitressing job while she awaited a chance shot at stardom that never came.

On January 15, 1947, her dismembered, disfigured corpse was discovered in a vacant lot in southern Los Angeles. Severed in half at the waist, her nude torso and legs were posed a foot apart; her arms spread above her head, legs profanely spread. Her body was clean and emptied of blood (indicating that it had been ritualistically cleaned and then dumped); and, perhaps most debasingly, she bore a bloody grimace, her face deformed into what's known as a

"Glasgow smile"—sliced from the corners of her lips to her ears. Her marred body was also afflicted with various cuts, lacerations, ligature marks, and bruises.

She was soon identified by her fingerprints, and although numerous suspects and persons of interest were brought forward and questioned over the years, her murderer was never found. Potential developments in the case have emerged as recently as 2013, when the San Bernadino *Sun* reported the investigation of George Hill Hodel, a deceased doctor and long-suspected serial killer implicated by his own son. His home has since been visited by various paranormal crews, who have purportedly recorded electronic voice phenomena—or EVP—within; the Dahlia's beautiful ghost has also been said to frequent the areas around Tinseltown where she was last seen.

More than forty-five years later, in 1993, to pay homage to the city's slain native daughter, the Medford Historical Society erected a stone marker near her one-time home on 153 Salem Street (since razed for an interstate rotary). The memorial, a plaque set into a large granite boulder near the roundabout, refers to her background in the city—including her time attending Medford High School—calling her "Medford's 'Black Dahlia,'" and identifying her killing as "one of the nation's most infamous and unsolved crimes.

"Her striking attractive features, jet black hair and penchant for dark attire earned her the name of 'The Black Dahlia,'" the shrine reads.

Whether the beautiful aspiring star has found her peace all these decades later only she can know—but like many victims of lurid killings, she remains much more famed in death than she ever could hope to be in life.

TOYS NEED REST, TOO

Suddenly, one day, they began to appear—a whimsical herd of curios.

Arranged in a fenced-in section of a scruffy field in idyllic Lincoln outside Boston, grass tickles their plastic and wooden haunches, small holes mar their molded frames, paint chips off their muzzles; their saddles are worn with use, springs creaky and rusted, fabric tattered and soiled, glue losing its adhesion, and wood grayed with the elements.

It is a fanciful graveyard of toys, a final resting place for a gathering of more than two dozen rocking horses.

It all started with just one or two, after a couple local kids set them up along with a lemonade stand several years ago, resident Harold McAleer told the *Boston Globe*. Over time, their pack has inexplicably thickened; one here, one there, at least one purple-maned unicorn tagging along in their midst.

"There was something lovely about it being anonymous," Elizabeth Graver, who owns the parcel of field on which the fillies prance, told the *Globe*.

And as their assembly has grown, their configuration has trotted and clomped around to accommodate: Unseen hands (it can be assumed) have organized them in large circles facing one another in a sort of pony powwow; arranged them side by side as if in a race with no outcome, forever biting at their bits in anticipation; gathered them around for a fantastical tea party.

And while they're not believed to be haunted—if they are, we can only hope it's with good memories—they serve as an idiosyncratic tribute to fleeting youth.

LIZZIE BORDEN TOOK A LEASH

Most of us are familiar with the grisly nursery rhyme detailing Lizzie Borden's penchant for axes and fatal whacks.

But in addition to her allegedly bloody ways, Fall River's so-called murderess had quite a doting side. Most notably, she was known to keep pets in her aging spinsterhood. In a dedication both eerie and eccentric given the Borden lore, three of Lizzie's cherished Boston terriers are interred in Pine Ridge Cemetery in the south-of-Boston town of Dedham, one of the state's few dedicated pet burial grounds. Set unassumingly against a stone wall, "Donald Stuart," "Royal Nelson," and "Laddie Miller" (one can only guess how the infamous acquitted murderer contrived their stately names) are memorialized with a simple pink granite stone. It is also carved with the family moniker and the peaceful epitaph, "Sleeping Awhile."

Rather at odds with her caricature as an ax-wielding butcher, Lizzie was quite the animal lover. It was her bequest upon her death to provide continuous financial support to the Faxon Animal Care and Adoption Center (formerly the Animal Rescue League of Fall River, which she helped to establish in 1913 by providing seed money), according to the *Chicago Tribune*.

"I have been fond of animals," she wrote in her will, "and their need is great and there are so few who care for them."

It's long been said that animals have the power to heal; apparently, in Lizzie's case, they also have the ability to melt a murderous heart (allegedly, that is).

AND WHILE WE'RE ON THE SUBJECT OF BELOVED PETS . . .

Those familiar with Stephen King's horrific novel *Pet Sematary*, a contemporary tale of necromancy gone awry (is there any other kind?), might be intrigued to explore the shrines to the furred, feathered, finned, and pawed in Boston's locality.

In addition to Pine Ridge, the country's oldest pet cemetery with a section dating to the early 1900s, there's Angel View Pet Cemetery and Crematory in Middleboro, also south of Boston, as well as Hillside Acre Animal Cemetery in Methuen just north of Boston.

The melancholy epitaphs, lush overgrowth, and somber, homemade remembrances will no doubt remind visitors of King's vision. Stones both simple and ornate serve as tributes to a panoply of the expected dog and cat companions, as well as horses, bunnies, and even lizards. Carved angel protectors, full-size statues, and realistic etchings, slate stones, flags, and flowers remember Cocos, Trixies, Otises, Roxies, Ragses, and Muffins, accompanied with epitaphs professing "Now my life is empty," "I love you sleepy head," "Small in stature, big in heart," and "You were part of our lives' greatest memories and milestones."

Just don't go poking around the back in search of a secret, mystical path guarded by the legendary "Wendigo."

TRULY MONUMENTAL

There's nothing quite as spooky as a vast, rolling, tree-laden necropolis embellished here and there with baroque structures, literal beds set among six-foot-deep eternal beds, tiny weathering villages, and effigies of children encased in transparent cases for perpetuity.

Founded in 1848, the 275-acre Forest Hills Cemetery in the Jamaica Plain "streetcar suburb" of Boston features some of the area's most intriguingly macabre funerary art.

First, after passing through its lavish spired gate, there are "Gracie" and "Louis," statues of children forever youthful and preserved in see-through containers. Louis, or more simply referred to as "the boy in the boat," memorializes the French-born Louis Ernest Mieusset, who died in 1886 before his fifth birthday. He sits infinitely perched on the edge of a small dinghy, one leg slung over the side. Dressed in genteel Victorian-era garb—head of curls, pleated frock, coat secured with a bow—he holds a tennis racquet in one hand, boot-clad foot dipped in the purling waves. According to the *Jamaica Plain Gazette*, it is a slightly unsettling homage to the final living moments of a *fils bien aime* ("well-beloved son"). Born in France in 1881, the boy's mother brought him to the States, where he met his premature end. As reported by the *Gazette,* on September 26, 1886, he drowned while trying to retrieve his pet rabbit on the nearby shore. The monument was also initially equipped with a marble bench with a drawer where his mother kept vigil and stored cleaning products for her son's shrine. Becoming poverty stricken in her old age, Madame Mieusset was at first buried in a pauper's grave, until a neighbor wrote to the mayor and she was disinterred and finally laid to rest beside her son.

The haunting of his grave is of a benevolent sort; for years, according to the *Gazette*, anonymous hands have regularly laid fresh flowers at his stone feet. (And more playfully, colorful action figures of superheroes the boy never knew or could fathom in his lifetime can be found lined up along the outside of his case—unfortunately just out of reach of his eternally enclosed hands.)

Not far away stands the idol of a potential playmate, "Gracie." Also gripped by death before cresting age five, Grace Sherwood Allen died in 1880 of whooping cough, a common ailment of the day, according to the Forest Hills Educational Trust. She is kept safe for the ages in a domed case, depicted in a frilly Victorian dress, bow in her hair, clasping a drooping bunch of flowers.

Both statues are eerily expressionless, kept immortally young in clear containers, the only sign of wear the oxidation in the way of black streaking their bronze frames.

Taking the metaphor of everlasting sleep literally, meanwhile, the burial ground features two realistic, true-to-size twin beds. Facing one another, pillows indented and sheets crumpled as if they were just moments before carelessly risen from, they are tarnished with black smears by merciless time. Stone pillows are hastily "strewn" beside them on the grass; their headboards are decorated with winged cherub amulets. In the end, they serve as a stark reminder of the taste of death we all get with each night's sleep.

In a touch of both whimsy and as a dedication to its permanent residents, local artist Christopher Frost cast miniature concrete buildings that dot a rocky outcropping in one section of the cemetery. Placed in 2006 and since overtaken by encroaching lichen and bright green mossy growth, they are replicas of the homes of some of Forest Hill's interred, ranging from farmhouses to modern split-levels to Queen Anne mansions, and are stamped with their professions in life: "lead manufacturer," "temperance leader," "merchant," "wagon driver."

Scattered above the stones of the departed here, they are a blunt indication of just how weighty the word "livelihood" is, throughout our lifetimes and following us in our deaths.

Elsewhere, there are winged, frocked angels looking to the heavens, stones with sleeping babies or final curtains draping down, life-sized stone canine protectors, and crosses smothered with flowers.

In the end (how fitting a transition . . .), Forest Hills emphasizes the notion that burial places—purportedly haunted or not—don't always have to be bleak or sterile homages to those who came before.

The same is true of renowned Mount Auburn Cemetery in Cambridge, a literal sculpture park and repository of art (as well the deceased). Founded in 1831 as America's first "garden cemetery"—meaning that it was intended as much for the pastoral enjoyment of the living as the peaceful rest of the dead—it makes an immediate impression with its Egyptian Revival gateway (the first structure of its kind in the United States). Constructed of Quincy granite, measuring sixty feet across and standing twenty-five feet tall, it features obelisks connected to a quartet of lodges and a cornice stone decorated with a drooping lotus and winged globe motifs.

Walk within it, where more than 60,000 monuments, both majestic and morose, sprawl across 175 acres. Most notable: a giant resting sphinx in an Egyptian headdress commemorating those who fell in the Civil War; an ornately spired Gothic Revival chapel; a round, open-air pillared shrine to Mary Baker Eddy, founder of the Christian Science religious movement; and a sixty-two-foot-tall Washington Tower with a spiral staircase, battlements, and a panoramic view of Boston. There are also cherub and angel protectors, life-sized dogs and bald eagles, Buddhist stupas (hemispherical structures that serve as refuges of meditation), life-sized statues of bereaved young women posed in prayer, boulders carved to appear as if they are stacked ever-so-precipitously one upon the other, Victorian-style tombs, ivy-roofed mausoleums, and graves topped with realistic fedoras that look as if they could be just plucked off and worn.

More heartbreakingly, some graves are emblazoned with grief-stricken poems and letters from left-behind loved ones. In a grim reminder of morbidity, meanwhile, a plot dedicated to the Wigglesworth family featuring a variety of exquisitely carved tombs also includes a realistic cradle for infant Mary Wigglesworth, who died in 1884 just shy of her second birthday. Carved of limestone, the bassinet is encrusted with the patina of the ages, gripped by moss, a creased pillow bearing an epitaph, a center bed where a baby should lie instead overgrowing with clover and wildflowers.

And although nearly all cemeteries have their purported restless spirits, sometimes it's the epitaphs they leave behind—reminiscences of pain, sorrow, severed connections, lost chances—that prove the most haunting.

Part 5

THE FORGOTTEN ONES

They were the discards, the left behind, cast away by society. Abandoned to wither and waste behind brick walls, left with their own cycle of thoughts inside clinical white rooms.

Insane asylums. State lunatic hospitals. Schools for the feebleminded. For such a small geographic area, Massachusetts, from the mid-1800s to the mid-1900s, had its allotment of these initially well-intentioned institutions for the mentally ill, the intellectually disabled, or the simply misunderstood. Built on the humane concept of "moral treatment" born of the Enlightenment in the eighteenth century, they inevitably became the repositories of inestimable pain and suffering, abhorrent conditions, and beastly practices that bred further sickness and madness.

By their very nature they were—and are—creepy and menacing locales. Many, at least for a time, were abandoned in turn, like their one-time residents—boarded over, bricked up, fenced in.

And both in their functioning years and in their ensuing solitude and silence, they have kindled many a ghastly and ghostly story.

Chapter 14

Asylum of Murder

Turn a corner and you are suddenly upon it: a derelict building, effaced by vandals, nature expressing its intent at reclamation with a slow but insistent creep across surrounding concrete paths and up its brick edifice. Park in a lot right beside it and take a walk around—the columned, steepled structure, identified in barely legible bas relief as the Dr. William F. McLaughlin Building, is an ominous, veritable fortress, every one of its entryways, rectangular windows, available crevasses, and draft spaces intentionally cleaved by hands or time, is welded shut or secured with layers of bricks or boards.

Horrifically photogenic, it could be something directly out of a horror movie—and, ultimately, it served as the site of a real-life horror, one that earned it the macabre nickname of the "Hospital of Seven Teeth."

The rectangular structure—as well as a sparse cemetery located a ways down the hill in the woods, a location you don't just happen upon but have to be actively on the lookout to find—is all that remains of the former Metropolitan State Hospital. Closed now for more than twenty years, it has since been significantly abbreviated of its once grandiose complex of seventeen buildings spread across 378 acres in Waltham, Belmont, and Lexington, suburbs just west of Boston.

Known locally as "the Met," it opened in 1930 to meet what was then considered a dire need for an additional psychiatric hospital in greater Boston (aiding several that were already long-established in Boston, Danvers, Worcester, Taunton, Tewksbury, and Foxborough).

Unlike other facilities for the mentally ill in the state and across the country, it was not based on the well-regarded Kirkbride layout but was instead designed in a Colonial Revival style by architect Gordon C. Robb, according to the Lexington Historical Commission. Its campus included a medical-surgical building, male and female dorms, a court-yard, auditorium, chapel, morgue, cemetery, administration building, and staff housing, as well as a sizeable "continuous treatment group" area for the most acute patients, com-prised of eight wings and a secured central courtyard. Close by, the Gaebler Children's Center—also now shuttered—served mentally ill boys and girls. Also not far away was the Walter E. Fernald State School, a sanitarium for boys with "low intelligence" that became notorious for its role in the eugenics movement, as well as wanton nuclear medical research, neglect, and physical and sexual abuse. (It finally closed in late 2014 after decades of legal battles.)

The Met was said to be as rambling below ground as it was above—an extensive series of tunnels ran underneath the hospital complex, serving as entrances, exits, bypasses, and connective corridors. Although since sealed shut—much like the institution's lone remaining building—they have been described by former employees as painted concrete corridors meagerly lit by bare bulbs and overrun by arrogant cockroaches, with off-shooting rooms housing various-sized cages, beds and chains.

In addition to rampant allegations of patient mistreat-ment, the hospital became infamous for a grisly, ritualis-tic murder that remained unsolved (or, some say, simply ignored) for years.

In 1978, lifetime mental patient Melvin Wilson killed fellow convalescent Anne Marie Davee. In his fifties and institutionalized for nearly forty years, according to reports at the time by the Associated Press, he was believed to use a hatchet to maim thirty-six-year-old Davee, burying pieces of her hacked-up body in three separate graves around a sloped, wooded area of the hospital grounds—and, perhaps most disturbingly, keeping at least seven of her teeth as mementos, which forensic examiners said he extracted post-humously. Following her disappearance, as reported by the *Boston Globe*, hospital employees found a hut where the two had apparently clandestinely met; they also later discovered a bundle containing a hatchet, a pocketbook, and pieces of women's clothing.

However, Davee remained missing for two years until 1980, when state senators opened up an investigation into "seclusion, restraint and deaths" at several state-supported mental hospitals, specifically focusing on nineteen cases, including Davee's. Months of scrutiny ensued, with accusations that Met hospital staff fed eager, pyromaniac patients lit cigarettes, punched and kicked them, painted swastikas on their bodies, and sexually assaulted them, according to the *Globe*. Other circulating rumors related to the nearby Gaebler complex told of several children who were accidentally fatally poisoned by a new medicine.

Not long after the exposed maltreatment there and elsewhere, the hospital closed in January 1992 as part of a broader statewide deinstitutionalization movement, according to the Lexington Historical Commission. And for fifteen years, it remained that way: abandoned, overtaken by its lush environs, overrun by squatters and vandals and youth seeking out a party place with the potential for a good spook. Then in 2007, a large portion was converted to luxury apartments known as Avalon at Lexington Hills. (Residential development is a common denouement for many a former institutional building and mill complex in congested New England.) Today, all that remains is the crumbling administration building, much of it surrounded by as-yet undeveloped overgrown land, as well as trails, open space, and woods that contain the hidden-away graveyard.

Perhaps not surprisingly, given the assemblage of lost and tortured souls it harbored over decades, paranormal phenomena were reported long before the hospital was shuttered. According to the New England Center for the Advancement of Paranormal Science, both staff and patients (many of the latter, it should be noted, under the influence of antipsychotic medications) reported hearing incorporeal screams in areas where electroshock therapy took place, and also said they witnessed shadowy figures suddenly appearing and then disappearing, passing through walls, or mysteriously showing up in rooms locked from the outside. Residents recently or long deceased were seen walking the halls or materializing in their old rooms, as well, and some workers claimed that while walking through the underground passageways, they were followed by ethereal whispers, and even touched by ghostly hands.

These days, as is the case with other spooky locales, visitors often report a feeling of being watched; some paranormal investigators have even claimed to have experienced the morose emotions and hopelessness of past patients, followed by the ability to recollect memories and recall painful, crude, scantly documented procedures in detail.

Others claim that the grounds are prowled by untold unnamed dead who never received a proper burial. The property's only marked cemetery takes effort to find; down the hill a few paces from the posh residential area is a trail head for the Western Greenway.

Follow a gravel path for three-quarters of a mile or so through trees and marsh, manhole covers beset at sporadic intervals hinting at the hospital's once-expansive grounds and infrastructure. Eventually, the trail opens up on the right—a rock wall rimming a large green rectangle, a stately tree standing at center. A sign erected by the Massachusetts Department of Conservation and Recreation informs you that this is Metfern Cemetery, which served as the site of 310 burials between 1947 and 1979 for both Metropolitan State Hospital and the Fernald School (clearly not representative of even a fraction of either institution's vast number of patients).

Tilted to and fro, askew, and cracked, they merely identify those who (ostensibly) lie beneath them with anonymous numbers, as well as a *P* or a *C* marking them as, respectively, Protestant or Catholic. (And visitors will no doubt notice the stark symbolism of the several yards of grassy paces that separate the two factions.)

Some stones have been swallowed so deep into the shifting earth that viewing them requires brushing aside clumps of recently cut grass; others are so washed out that only a tracing finger can determine their allotted number and religious designation.

Ultimately, the burial ground is far larger than the number of stones it bears—prompting one to wonder how many are interred in unmarked plots here and elsewhere on the hospital's once ample grounds.

Still, whatever secrets and mysteries it holds will remain that way, forever hidden away (or at least until it is demolished or rehabbed).

Make a visit to the administration building, located along a windy byway just off one of Waltham's main drags. Flanked by the new residential complex that took much of its place and dominates the nearby hill, the three-story structure is absorbed by weeds and other overgrowth, in some cases up to its battened second-story windows. Sporadic signs warn of asbestos within. Ivy curls its delicate fingers along brick edges and corners, creating flourishing paths all the way to the lip of its shingled roof, or trailing its way like verdant ornamentation up handrails to what was once a dignified front entrance.

Walk up the concrete stairway, steps marked with squiggles of black spray paint—watching your step for ankle-wrenching rifts in the stone or potentially tetanus-inflicting rusty nails jutting jaggedly out of errant boards. The once-white paint on the four pillars and the portico around and above you has grayed and been casually flicked away by the elements. The landing in front of the barricaded metal door is a farrago of splintered wood, chunks and shards of slate and concrete, plastic buckets, sullied blankets; a green office chair, stuffing exposed, lies strewn on its back amid a pile of rubble to one side of the stone steps.

Curlicues of graffiti, both obscene and indiscernible, cover nearly every reachable surface. The sealed metal door, two locks on it mangled, is marred by deep gouges and dents from the insistent and frustrated efforts of vandals. Entries around back are similarly barred and gashed; one cobwebby hole was successfully extracted—but probe it with your fingers and the only mysteries within are further layers of boards and the pungent smell of mildew and decay.

Walking away, one can only wonder: Were such measures taken to keep intruders out? Or hem resident specters in?

Chapter 15
Ruthless Abandon

Morphine, atropine, strychnine—they were all potions of pleasure for the well-regarded nurse. After injecting her unsuspecting victims with varying levels of lethal doses, it was said that Jane Toppan climbed into what ultimately became their deathbeds, embracing them, kissing them, admittedly deriving sexual satisfaction out of their final convulsions and spasms.

They called her "Jolly" Jane. Quite the misnomer.

Toppan, a spinster who grew up in Lowell and "cared for" the sick and infirm at several area hospitals at the turn of the twentieth century, confessed to killing thirty-one people over the course of ten years—although, by her own informal account, it could have been more than three times that—earning her the nickname the "Angel of Death." One of history's few female serial killers, she is also believed to be one of its most prolific—although experts on her case say she didn't achieve the disrepute of, say, John Wayne Gacy or "the Night Stalker" Richard Ramirez because her killings were of a more subdued sort, not involving sharp weapons, mangled bodies, or copious amounts of blood (she killed like a lady, you could say).

The nurse-turned-murderer-turned-mental-patient was one of the most notorious residents of Taunton State Hospital—a fitting union for a woman and a location both with ghastly, inhumane histories.

Originally known as the State Lunatic Hospital at Taunton, Massachusetts's second asylum for the mentally unstable opened in 1854 on a 154-acre farm separated from the main area of the south-of-Boston city by a river. Designed by eminent Worcester architect Elbridge Boyden in a Neoclassical style, with red brick, cast iron, a main dome, cupolas, and cornices, it was modeled on the plans of Philadelphia physician and advocate for the mentally ill, Dr. Thomas Story Kirkbride. Its most characteristic architectural feature was a curved, enclosed walkway with arched floor-to-ceiling windows (fodder for many a stylistic photo over the years by trespassing shutterbugs, paranormal researchers, and habitués of abandoned places). It was expanded on over the years, and at one time, it comprised as many as forty structures.

But within just a few years of admitting its first patient, or so the rampant stories go, the odious practices began—and they made Toppan look like Florence Nightingale compared to Nurse Ratched.

Most of the rumors center around satanic activity: In the mid-to-late 1800s, several nurses and doctors were purportedly members of a bloody cult (although this claim is not known to be either investigated or substantiated). They were said to drag numerous protesting patients to the basement or out to the surrounding woods, where they were then silenced during satanic rituals, as well as to regularly perform particularly brutal experiments involving shock treatment, blood baths, and even Frankenstein-like surgery where limbs were removed from one patient and grafted onto another, as noted by Nicholas Goodwin in *Spooky Creepy Boston*. In other stories, patients were boiled alive or chopped to pieces when they attempted to flee; many missing persons were also said to be last seen near the grove by the hospital.

In later years, both staff and residents claimed to feel the residual effects of these crimes: There were reports of an unseen presence that barred them from the basement, as well as sightings of a shadowy man who could crawl along the walls with ease and would stop to stare at patients.

As part of the state's defunding of state mental hospitals in the latter half of the twentieth century, Taunton was largely emptied and in disuse by the mid-1970s. As the result of its dereliction, its central dome collapsed in 1999, and a conflagration in 2006 leveled several of the historic sections of the property. Demolition followed in 2009, although several of the newer buildings remain today.

As do, some say, more than a few unexplainable presences.

Agonized moans and screams have been persistently reported in the adjacent woods; electric devices of all kinds have consistently failed on or near the site. Some have claimed to see various apparitions fleeing the area (perhaps for perpetuity, with no chance of escape), or, in particular, a man in either a patient's gown or a lab coat running pell-mell across the open farmland, according to Goodwin. Others have distinctly heard voices telling them, "Flee! Any way possible! As quickly as you can!"

Back when the oldest buildings were still standing (if idly), meanwhile, inexplicable lights were seen flicking on and off inside—and, more alarmingly, bloody hands were said to claw at the barred windows.

Then there was "Jolly" Jane herself.

The forty-five-year-old murderess was committed to Taunton State Hospital in 1902, and was confined there for thirty-six years.

Born Honora Kelley to Irish immigrant parents in 1857, she seemed blighted by the cloak of death from the very start. Her mother was claimed by "consumption" (tuberculosis); her father by alcoholism and mental illness. A tailor by trade, the paterfamilias reportedly turned his tools gruesomely on himself: Peter Kelley was found in his shop attempting to sew his own eyes shut and was summarily institutionalized.

Young Honora was sent to an orphanage, then sold into a form of indentured servitude—as was a custom at the time with impoverished immigrants—to the Toppan family of Lowell. Although never formally adopted, she took their surname and the given name Jane.

She was described as both a brilliant and aggressive child, according to a story in the *Lowell Sun* newspaper, with a penchant for stealing, lying, and making up grandiose stories about her family history. She purportedly endured verbal barbs slung by her adoptive mother, and, as is often the case with young women growing up alongside one another, was also said to harbor a deep jealousy of her much more attractive and endearing foster sister, Elizabeth.

However, catty resentfulness typically doesn't end in merciless murder: Elizabeth was one of her sister's many victims, given a poisoned potion to sip on when Jane served as her temporary caretaker years later.

Because of her status as an indentured servant, as well as a chubby figure and a gruff demeanor, she was not popular among boys or young men—although in a well-circulated image, she appears as a handsome, full-figured woman, dark hair pulled back, eyebrows pensive lines, the faintest hint of a smile. She was said to be engaged once as a teenager, but was jilted when her beau left town and became enamored with another young woman (a turn of events that, it was asserted, sent her into a suicidal spiral).

After graduating from Lowell High School—and, upon her eighteenth birthday, being given fifty dollars by the Toppans as part of her servitude agreement—she worked for her adoptive family for a time, according to the *Sun*, then left the city with its thrumming mills for Cambridge in 1885 to train as a nurse.

As is the case with many serial murderers, the persona she portrayed to the public was vastly contradictory to the private one she long concealed. She arrived at Cambridge Hospital with a chipper and outgoing demeanor that earned her the nickname "Jolly" Jane, designated by her patients by which she was (very mistakenly, as many of them would learn in their last conscious moments) beloved.

And it didn't take long for her to begin experimenting with her deadly potions.

Changing up drugs and dosages—"Jolly" Jane was quite the tinkerer—she embarked on a silent binge of slayings that lasted more than a decade: patients, landlords, roommates, acquaintances; administering injections or enemas, feeding them pills, giving them poison-laced drinks. Most often she mixed the drugs morphine and atropine, which had wildly contradictory effects: The former would sedate her victims and make them lapse into comas, while the latter could send them into a deranged, capricious state. She combined the two narcotics to varying degrees, watching the results of different levels and timings of dosages and interactions. (The ever-shifting process also helped to mask her malicious deeds, with no distinct pattern and deviating symptoms and states of death that confounded medical examiners.)

In a few cases, she would treat patients as lab rats—and then nurse them back to health to get the rush of being a savior. But most often, she derived what she described as a "delirious enjoyment" and a "voluptuous delight" from the process, during which she would often hug her prey close to her stout body, nuzzling and caressing them, watching with rapture as they lapsed into comas and psychoses, bucking and twitching against the heavy veil of death that was enwrapping them.

Like a spider, Toppan targeted the weak and frail, those who wouldn't be missed or who possessed something she coveted. Along with her killing, she also continued her lifelong habits of lying and thievery—somehow continuously evading apprehension even as her peers came to loathe and distrust her.

Until, as is the undoing of many a miscreant, she got cocky and careless, decimating an entire Cape Cod family over a period of just two months. After being dismissed from both Cambridge Hospital and Massachusetts General Hospital, she became a private nurse, continuing her calculated killings, including that of her long-despised sister—since married—in 1899, as well as her housekeeper.

Two years later, in July 1901, landlord Mattie Davis paid Toppan what would be her final earthly visit; she had come to collect several hundred dollars in debt that the nurse owed on a summer home in the Cataumet section of Bourne, an ocean town tucked along the tricep of the Cape's arm. Toppan offered the woman a drink after her thirty-plus-mile trip by buggy—and within a week, the woman was dead.

Brashly moving in with the family following the funeral, Toppan next targeted Davis's youngest daughter, Genevieve Gordon. The young woman died in her bed in what many assumed was either a suicide or agony over her mother's sudden death. Patriarch Alden Davis was next, then his daughter Minnie Gibbs, who might as well have immediately gorged on her own morphine tablets when she refused Toppan's request to sign off on the debt she owed the family.

That vexing problem dealt with, the "jolly" nurse returned to Lowell, where she hoped to seduce her sister's widower.

But she left suspicions—and evidence literally unearthed in toxicology reports when the bodies of the decimated family were exhumed—behind. By October, she was arrested for Gibbs's slaying.

The story of the "Nightmare Nurse" and the "Angel of Death," as she was dubbed, soon enthralled and horrified the country. She showed no remorse for her deeds, instead confessing to them in stark detail and plainly stating, "My ambition is to have killed more people—helpless people— than any other man or woman who ever lived."

She even went so far as to offhandedly fault her spinster-hood for her lethal ways. "If I had been a married woman," she professed in a printed confession, according to the *Sun*, "I probably would not have killed all of those people. I would have had my husband, my children and my home to take up my mind." (Because, apparently, matrimony has the ability to quell murderous compunctions.)

In June 1902, after confessing to thirty-one murders— which she later said could have been as high as one hundred, although she, herself, even lost track—Toppan was found not guilty by reason of insanity. The jury deliberated for just under a half hour, according to the *Sun*; she was sentenced to Taunton State for life.

But even she begged to differ on that point. "She said she could not help committing the crimes," read a *New York Times* article from June 25, 1902. "She argued, moreover, that she was not insane. She said she knew what she was doing when she administered poison to her victims, and she asked Judge (Fred M.) Bixby how, under such circumstances she could be of unsound mind."

Nevertheless, she was locked away in Taunton for the next three-and-a-half decades, buried upon her death, according to the *Boston Globe*, in a pauper's grave beneath marker number 984 (long since disappeared—perhaps someone's macabre souvenir) in the city's Mayflower Hill Cemetery.

During her stay at the asylum, she allegedly attempted suicide and also starved herself at various periods.

Paranoid, it was said, that the nurses might be trying to poison her.

Chapter 16

Dreadful Sessions

It's a humid summer morning. After getting a bit turned around trying to find your way, you locate the gravel path you've been searching for. Avoiding gullies cleaved by voracious runnels from a recent rainstorm, you pass by hollow shells of new construction, their insides clanging and buzzing with activity. A catcall of "Don't do it!" serves as a playful attempt to dissuade you from venturing toward your creepy destination not far beyond the Gothic, red-brick clock tower. Crossing a small field of corn and ducking under the drooping boughs of trees that have long served as dutiful sentries, you enter a small enclosed clearing.

And, there, you literally stand alone among a company of the clinically insane.

Well—dozens and dozens of the *dead* insane, that is. (You can determine which is more unsettling. . . .)

The recently restored graveyard—just off public walking paths at Halstead Danvers, the luxury residential development twenty miles north of Boston—is the last remaining vestige of Danvers State Hospital, one of the country's most infamous asylums.

Known locally simply as "Kirkbride," the long-standing sanatorium was said to be tainted from the start by the dark, pervasive stain of the Salem witch trials. For years, it was reputed to be the site where the repulsive practice of prefrontal lobotomies either originated or were perfected (although there is negligible evidence to support this). It was also exposed for its heinous, diabolical early twentieth-century methods and conditions, and, prior to the razing and gutting of the near-entirety of its campus, its crumbling, chilling interiors and grand Gothic exteriors were immortalized in the 2001 modern cult horror classic *Session 9*.

Today, like the former Metropolitan State Hospital, it has been rehabbed into upscale housing, overlooking nearby Boston and Interstate 95 from its perch on a hilltop. But its memories remain, indelible imprints on the crest of land it has commanded for nearly 140 years.

Costing more than one million dollars to erect and spanning 70,000 square feet, the sprawling hospital complex was built in Danvers in 1878 over several hundred acres known as Hathorne Hill—named for the callous Salem judge John Hathorne who once inhabited it.

A Gothic, three-story, castle-like structure of red brick and granite, with numerous spires and gables, it stood on its promontory as an exotic oddity amid the area's prevailing Colonial and Colonial Revival building styles.

Eminent Boston architect Nathaniel J. Bradlee modeled the campus on the widely distributed plan developed by Dr. Thomas Kirkbride. Since inevitably taking on its progenitor's name, the design has served as a widespread archetype for asylums across the country, many of which have since been listed on the National Register of Historic Places.

Based on a moralistic, disciplining method of treatment, the Kirkbride model segregated patients according to their gender and severity of illness. In Danvers's case it took the form of a central building connected to tiers of several distinct wards on either side, so that from an aerial perspective, it resembled a jagged semicircle. (Over the years, other stand-alone structures were added as deemed by necessity.)

Beneath it, as was the case with the Met and other large institutional complexes in the area, underground channels traced a labyrinthine path.

At first, its staff was supposedly disdainful of restraints and other harsh treatment methods, so patients were allowed to roam at their leisure. But overcrowding, coupled with "advancements" in psychiatry, soon drastically changed things at Kirkbride on the hill.

As humans are known to habitually oversimplify out of convenience or misunderstanding, the institution at Danvers (as was the case on a widespread scale) became a catch-all receptacle for not only the legitimately mentally unbalanced and incapacitated but those who today would trend across various spectrums, as well as the vagrant, destitute, and misfits who simply had no other place in society.

What was initially built to house 450 patients was teeming with 2,000 or more by the 1940s (ultimately lending credence to the term "madhouse"). Desperate for room, staff allegedly put some of them up in congested attics and basements, and began implementing excruciating practices. In addition to the use of sedative drugs, straitjackets, and padded cells, residents both acute and chronic were said to be subjected to solitary confinement, shock therapy, hydrotherapy (in which they were immersed in tubs of water of varying temperatures for hours, nights, or days at a time depending on symptoms), forced into insulin shock or feverish states, and, most intrusively, submitted to lobotomies. The procedure—which at first was deemed revolutionary, its originator even receiving a long-contentious Nobel Prize—involves either invasive surgery or the insertion of a long, icepick-like implement known as an "orbitoclast" through the eye socket into the frontal lobe. (Spoiler alert: The torturous instrument is used as a killing method in *Session 9*.)

In keeping with the impersonal, stilted nature that came to define the care of the unruly populace, when patients died, they were either buried in unmarked graves in a field below the hospital or given a cold, anonymous grave with just a numbered marker. The numerals bore no more significance than to identify the order in which they died—a morbid assembly line of sorts. Virtually forgotten in life—even more anonymous in death.

Further claims of delinquency centered around short-handed staff who withheld or simply forgot food, water, and proper medication. A few patients were also said to sleep on bare floors or in broiling rooms, or were left unattended to wander naked, soil themselves, and sit fetid in their own waste.

Other unknowns were said to walk Kirkbride, as well.

Specifically, according to the research of Danvers archivist Richard B. Trask, many staff and patients over the years believed that the original main steeple—removed in April 1970 for safety reasons and replaced within the past ten years with a replica—was prowled by a phantom, particularly on stormy nights.

But as time drew on—and funding for state asylums was systematically whittled—a dwindling effect occurred, with patients released to other facilities, families, or more intimate residential settings better fitting their needs. Phase-out programs began in the 1970s, according to Trask.

By 1992, Danvers State Hospital was unceremoniously closed. And for more than a decade it sat that way, brooding and consigned to its hill.

Although its tough brick exterior remained largely sound, its interior decayed—tagged with spray paint, cement steps cracked straight in half as if under an immense weight, floors giving way to gravity, doors freeing themselves of rusty hinges, layers of paint simply abandoning decorum by spooling and rippling off the walls, photos and drawings that served as personalized wallpaper in patient rooms curled into scrolls and blanched by the sun. Detritus was everywhere; no one bothered to clean up with the exodus—chairs and bookcases were overturned; cabinets left open, patient files—telling of innermost secrets, phobias, compulsions, incriminations—strewn around like lurid confetti; tarnished stretchers and bed frames, stained bathtubs, rotted empty suitcases serving as grim relics; dates, drawings and scrawlings of nonsensical phrases and random, plucked words functioning as hieroglyphs of scattered minds.

And as above, so below: Down the hill, the graves of the anonymous dead were even more relinquished, stones tumbled and cracked, lost among hip-high fields of grass gone to seed, overtaken by the greedy reach of saplings and brambles.

Over the years, ghost hunters, thrill seekers, defilers, and petty arsonists were frequently arrested on-site—some identifying themselves to police with the last name X, according to police logs—prompting regular patrols by local law enforcement and, at least for a time, twenty-four-hour, state-employed guards.

Because of the high security, the site wasn't nearly as plumbed by paranormal researchers as other supposedly haunted locales. But the curious who did successfully venture inside had more than wreckage to report; there were tales of unworldly clanking, whirling noises, approaching and receding footsteps, lights emanating from no identifiable source, taunting voices, and anguished screams. But mostly, visitors recalled feeling a heavy emotional weight or a deeply distressing state, as if sensing the resonant suffering of the building and its one-time residents.

In 2001, *Session 9* was released, elevating the deserted mental hospital to a cultlike status. Shot almost entirely on-site, the low-budget psychological thriller directed by Connecticut native Brad Anderson follows a small asbestos-removal team that underbids (and ultimately wins) a contract to clean up the vacated premises. Kirkbride, hauntingly atmospheric in its decrepitude, plays a prominent role, serving as a de facto character—its commanding bedraggled exterior, crumbling gym, hallways with flaking walls, fenced-in stairwells, rooftop offering a vantage of the Boston skyline, and dusky, imprisoning tunnels setting a dark and cryptic aura for the drama.

But in addition to being haunted by the enigmatic former asylum, the film was said to also be inspired by a loathsome, real-life local murder (spoiler alert number 2). In 1995, financial analyst Richard Rosenthal killed his wife, Laura Jane, in their Cambridge backyard, beating her with a rock, then impaling her heart and lungs on a stake, according to various local and national newspaper reports. The supposed impetus? Her complaints that he had burned their ziti dinner. He was convicted the following year and sentenced to life in prison without parole.

Still, *Session 9* wasn't Kirkbride's first shot at notoriety; the former psychiatric facility was purportedly the inspiration for Arkham Sanitarium in H. P. Lovecraft's story "The Thing on the Doorstep." The famed Providence-based horror writer also referred to it by name in a few of his other tales for which he became posthumously revered.

Despite Kirkbride's prominence—locally, historically, architecturally, and in popular culture—it was sold by the state to Virginia-based AvalonBay Communities Inc. in December 2005 for eighteen million dollars, according to the *Boston Globe*. Despite delays from permit holdups and court challenges by local preservationists, much of the original complex was subsequently demolished and replaced.

The long-obscured burial ground, meanwhile, quite literally had to be stumbled upon to be rediscovered. An ex-patient activist was walking her dog on the rambling, vacated campus one spring afternoon in 1997 when she suddenly happened upon several of the numbered markers in two distinct areas. They were so embedded in dense thicket that they—and the distressed souls they harbored—were nearly misplaced to eternity. Years of work by a grassroots group of ex-patients and others, the Danvers State Memorial Committee, helped to give names to—and, it can only be hoped, ultimately placate—the abandoned dead. It was consecrated with a ceremony in 2002 in which hundreds of patient names were read off with the accompanied ringing of a bell. The effort, according to the committee, required intensive research and interviews, as the original cemetery ledger had been lost years earlier.

But in what some attribute to the prevalent evil of Hathorne—who was known for his penchant for torture and was so scorned following the trials that his family temporarily buried him in his dirt cellar to prevent vandals from defiling his body—construction of the now hundreds of high-end apartments and condos on the site was hampered by a four-alarm fire in April 2007. According to reports in the local newspaper, the *Salem News*, three new buildings were destroyed and others badly damaged, smoke was so heavily cloaking that the nearby highway had to be temporarily closed, and the embers of the riotous blaze took several days to fully extinguish.

Today, though, as you wend your way up to the top of Kirkbride Drive past the numerous deluxe residences—including several under construction—you'd hardly know it was once the location of such anguish and calamity. The weather-vane-topped central tower that now serves as the administration building is flanked on both sides by Gothic cupolas and trusses rising above the copse of trees.

Down the hill a ways, the entrance to the tucked-away, unassuming graveyard of the insane is marked by a large boulder; its solemn epitaph hints at the wrongs endured by its dead: "The Danvers State Hospital Cemetery—The Echos [*sic*] They Left Behind."

Follow a damp, grass-spotted path into a sun-spattered dale bordered by a stone wall and a cracked, collapsing fence bereft of many of its pickets, vines vigorously clambering over its side.

To the left: A black stone monument dedicated to "Nobody's Child" Marie Rose Balter, a hospital resident from 1948 to 1968. At the clearing's center: A bench and three stone markers listing hundreds of patients, along with their dates of birth and death and the apologetic sentiment, "With love, we remember your names." Perhaps fittingly, given the history of this place, it is ornamented with the remnants of a funerary wreath, the moldered Styrofoam oval drooping with flowers that are far advanced beyond a state of decomposition to near mummification.

The oldest born a generation before the War of the Rebellion that cleaved the country in half, hundreds of former patients lie beneath flat rectangular stones dotting the mild slope in neat rows, the silence of their abiding sleep interspersed with the guttural cawing of crows, the clatter of nearby construction, and the constant murmur of the nearby highway. At the peripheries of the resting place, some names and numbers have been united—including Number 1, Frank Lawrence (1826–1878), and Number 120, Mary Ann Swift (1865–1888).

Elsewhere, the simple rectangular pillars or mere baseball-sized disks set into the ground reflect the generations of aspersion: Some are covered with dirt that requires a dusting hand to read them, others encroached by grass, still more are nearly swallowed up, literally sinking into the ground. They are spread about sporadically—"25," "299," "444" (unknowingly to its bearer, made famous by *Session 9*, in which one of the team listens to the reel-to-reel tapes of a "patient 444," the multiple-personality-afflicted Mary Hobbes). Sympathetic hands, meanwhile, propped "559" up against a tree and dangled a set of colorful rosary beads just above it.

As a further reminder of past neglect, the old markers—hexagon-topped concrete posts with metal-stamped numbers that stood sentinel here for decades over nameless dead—yet remain. Toward the bottom right of the grounds, just a step or two into the woods, dozens of them are haphazardly strewn and stacked. Overtaken by moss, swarmed with ivy, cracked or halved, exposed of their interior rebars, numbers (rising into the high 500s) tarnished or chipped off, leaving barely readable silhouettes just a few shades darker than the underlying concrete.

They are, quite fittingly, now forgotten themselves.

Despite the burial ground's resurrection (forgive the suitably eerie descriptor), finding it still requires a hunt, even for those aware and on the lookout—so in a way, those who lie here are still shunned, hidden-away vestiges of a dark past.

Although not known to be haunted in the traditional sense—but dare to take a walk there on a dark night and find out?—the reverberations of its history are haunting enough.

Chapter 17
History on Display

While most of the once state-funded hospitals have since been retrofitted into housing—garnering many a headline from local newspapers along the lines of "You'd have to be crazy to live there" (or not to)—and others that do remain vacant are barred up and entry prohibited, there are those that actually welcome exploration.

For instance, Tewksbury State Hospital (to sound like a local, pronounce it "Tooksbury," like something you'd snatch), portions of which are still a functioning health facility, offers a walking tour in the summer. Those seeking further exploration can make the trek to one of the site's three burial grounds that are said to be filled with more than 10,000 dead. Pines Cemetery, fittingly named, appears as just a thicket; but look closer at the pine-needle-and-leaf-strewn forest floor and you'll notice the small metal markers. Simple numbered laurel wreaths inset with crosses, they are embedded and rusted to varying degrees, jutting just a few inches out of the undergrowth.

Established in 1854 as a state almshouse for the poor, Tewksbury State Hospital—also known for a time as the Massachusetts State Infirmary—soon accepted what were known as the "pauper insane," and facilities were added on over the years to house patients afflicted with various infectious diseases. One of its most famous residents was Anne Sullivan, who, although she contracted the eye disease trachoma as a child, came to distinguish herself as one of the most eminent representatives of those with disabilities. Like the aforementioned "Jolly" Jane, she was born to immigrant parents and orphaned at a young age—her mother died, her father abandoned her and her brother, so she ended up in the Tewksbury "poor house"—but unlike the infamous slaughterer Toppan, she transformed her destitution into a good, becoming a teacher and close friend to the famed and revered Helen Keller.

The grounds also house the country's first public health museum, filled with some disturbingly experimental contraptions that evolved with medical advancements. Located in the Richard Morris building, or the old administration complex, its entry is eerily picturesque: Stone gates bridged by a simple wrought iron cutout sign frame the gabled, turreted red-brick structure dominated by a central steeple. Opened in 1994, according to the museum's website, it has exhibits on patent medicines, polio, and tuberculosis. Some of its artifacts include antique wooden wheelchairs, an iron lung, clunky leg braces, buckled restraints, pharmaceutical log books bloated with water damage and browned with age, superannuated medicine bottles (such as Varnesis from 1916 for rheumatism, containing "not over 15 percent alcohol"), nursing gowns and uniforms for patient baseball teams, and primitive dental apparatus and tools that would inspire odontophobia in even the most laid-back of patients.

Amid its historical setting, the old asylum serves as a reminder of the trial-and-error processes, procedures and treatments (some of them, as previously noted, downright grisly and gruesome) that those confined here were subjected to – and that no doubt compounded afflictions of mind and body that already served as curses of a lifetime.

Part 6

DISTURBED DEAD

Some spirits—whether by choices of their own or the actions of others—just can't seem to find that eternal, promised rest.

Chapter 18

An Eerie Process

Stooping and squinting as he methodically worked to develop the daguerreotype, the amateur photographer suddenly halted, perplexed.

As William H. Mumler had arranged it, the 1861 self-portrait depicted him seated against a simple backdrop, dressed in formal dark clothing.

But as the image began to take form, lights and darks and silhouettes settling into their assigned places, something else began to appear. Something that hadn't been there at the time the cumbersome shutter finally clicked, something airy and light and flowing, strange and completely unexpected.

Behind him in the portrait, seemingly floating over his left shoulder, was what appeared to be a female form. Faint, features unrefined—but, nevertheless, there.

Initially, he dismissed it—this was the 1860s when photography development was still a delicate and unrefined procedure, after all, and he was a dabbler whose main profession was engraving. It was likely a trace image from a previously processed plate, he told himself, some kind of trick of light, the result of overexposure or underexposure.

Still, he couldn't dismiss the intriguing image. At the encouragement of his friends, he gave it a closer inspection.

And this time there was no doubt.

The girl flanking him wasn't a fluke of exposure or the mechanism, or a lingering imprint left behind by a previous shoot. He immediately recognized it as his cousin—who had died twelve years prior.

Before long, he was replicating the process for friends and family—and, soon, paying customers.

News of his supposed otherworldly photo circulated throughout the spiritualist community, a growing faction during a time of so much despair and death, when men—young, old, fathers, sons—were falling in battle by the thousands and their sorrowful, vulnerable family members, lovers, and friends were desperate for closure.

Mumler's self-portrait became widely accepted as the first known image depicting an alleged ghost. Thus began his accidental (or, as some who believed he held a gift, destined) career—prolific, lucrative, exciting praise and adulation that were as loud as his detractors' cries of fraud and deception—capturing the supposed fleeting likenesses of the dead.

Boston, among its many other firsts, can claim the phenomenon that soon came to be known as "spirit photography."

From his studio on Boston's Washington Street, Mumler captured a range of ethereal, eerie, moving, and disquieting images, charging the exorbitant sum of ten dollars apiece at a time when typical portraits were a nickel or less, as noted by Holly Mascott Nadler in *Ghosts of Boston Town*.

They depict a range of men and women, posing somber in anticipation, ghostly figures standing behind and beside them in various states of corporeality. Hazy forms of children extend their hands to their mothers; profiles of lovers, siblings, and parents drape their arms around unsuspecting chests, rest their palms on shoulders, or seem to meld with and overlap their one-time human companions, as if attempting to blend souls; silhouettes stand near or far, simply hulking. They range from crisp and fully formed—down to the detailed ringlets of their hair and the lined and weary looks on their faces—to mere blurry outlines, traces of shadows, nondescript lines that barely apportion themselves from the atmosphere around them.

But one image in particular—which is still circulated today—secured Mumler's infamy. After relocating from Boston to New York in 1869 (following the paths of many who seek fame and success in one of America's most influential cities), he was visited at his studio by a short and squat middle-aged woman identifying herself as Mrs. Tydall (or Mrs. Tundall in some accounts of the story), wearing all black, face concealed by a veil.

Patiently waiting as Mumler did his work, she was said to remove her disguise just before the shutter closed, then promptly covered herself once more before leaving.

When her unassuming photographer set to developing the image, he was awestruck: His subject was none other than former first lady Mary Todd Lincoln, who, after losing two sons prior to the assassination of her husband, had long been rumored to have an interest in the occult and methods of rousing the dead.

In the photo, the distinguished presidential wife is accompanied by the unmistakable likeness of Abraham Lincoln; his towering form stands behind her, hands clasping her shoulders. Slightly behind him is a much less substantial form: a barely tangible torso with a bulbous, hairless, featureless head.

But in addition to drawing the curious and stalwart in their belief, Mumler was greeted with just as much scrutiny and ire. Prominent photographers and politicians investigated him, following his processes, step by step—in a few cases, as a result, becoming transformed into believers—and he was eventually brought up on several charges, among them fraud, larceny, and obtaining money under false pretenses, according to Mascott Nadler.

A sensational trial—questioning the very legitimacy of spirit photography itself—commenced. Mumler's defense argued that he had an irrefutable gift that reunited the living and the dead, and called numerous witnesses whose deceased loved ones had been "captured" in his photographs.

But the prosecution blisteringly accused Mumler of fakery, arguing that he knowingly preyed on susceptible victims despondent in their grief and their desire to make amends and offer final good-byes to loved ones. Legendary showman P. T. Barnum, holding true to his "there is a sucker born every minute" adage, took up the cause against Mumler, working with a photographer to fake a spirit photograph spoofing the Lincoln image—it shows him in profile, the blatant iconic profile of the sixteenth president peering over his shoulder.

Darkroom specialists were also brought forward to testify that such photos could be manipulated through double exposure. Other more blatant methods could involve outright deception, according to the prosecution—because those posing for photos at the time were required to sit without moving for up to a minute as the camera's shutter remained open, a second figure could easily tiptoe in without them knowing and remain for a short while, inevitably creating a blurry shimmer that could resemble a ghost.

Ultimately, though, Mumler was acquitted due to a lack of evidence—spectral or otherwise—although his career was decidedly destroyed. With both sides claiming victory, the outcome did nothing to dissuade imposters; so-called spirit photography only flourished.

Still, whether real or fake, Mumler's images continue to circulate, serving as a reminder of humankind's perpetual yearning to bridge the recesses between the living and the dead.

Chapter 19

The Peculiar John Hammond

Some people can simply afford to be eccentric—whether in life or in death.

John Hays Hammond Jr., the prolific nineteenth-century inventor who built an unrivaled palatial home on Gloucester's craggy coast, was dedicated to advancing daily life—as well as his own life in the hereafter.

Although his name doesn't quite evoke the same iconic image as Thomas Edison—the progenitor of, among many other things, such modern mainstays as long-lasting electricity, recorded music, and moving pictures—Hammond was just as abundant with ideas over his seventy-seven years. Best known for creating the remote control (a device that many a twenty-first-century inhabitant of the first world would be loath to live without) he came up with eight-hundred-plus inventions that led to more than four hundred patents.

To this day, he remains second to Edison when it comes to awarded patents—albeit a distant runner-up; the godfather of invention holds a record-setting 1,093, according to the Edison Innovation Foundation—and was so well-respected for his ideas and enthusiasm that he was a regular correspondent and protégé to both the so-called Wizard of Menlo Park and the father of the practical telephone, Alexander Graham Bell. It was said that he was even initially inspired to invent after a trip to Edison's workshop at the impressionable age of twelve.

Born in San Francisco in 1888 to wealthy mining engineer John Hays Hammond Sr., he spent a significant amount of his young life in England, where he became enraptured with the architecture, history, and lore of castles. In an unpublished letter, he wrote that "it is in the stones and wood that the personal record of man comes down to us. We call it atmosphere, this indescribable something that still haunts old monuments . . . it is a marvelous thing, this expression of human ideals in walls and windows."

Upon locating in the prosperous, north-of-Boston maritime city of Gloucester in the 1920s, he set out to infuse his own ideals—both earthly and not—in architecture. In 1926, work began on his namesake Hammond Castle, a medieval-inspired structure with buttresses, turrets, pillars, arches, grottoes, cupolas, towers, vast halls, and passages, that stands stately along Gloucester's rock-ribbed shore.

When it was completed in 1929, Hammond thus dubbed it Abbadia Mare, or "Abbey by the Sea," and complemented its architectural opulence with his immense collection of artifacts spanning Roman, medieval, and Renaissance eras.

Today a privately owned museum listed on the National Register of Historic Places, the grand property features halls beset with European storefronts, innate arched courtyards traced with local flora, drawbridges, pools, elaborate staircases, fireplaces, intricate stained-glass windows, walls embedded with ancient tombstones and Roman sarcophagi, and a panoply of artifacts, from chests, to organs, to six-hundred-year-old beds.

Upon moving to the magnificent estate with his wife Irene, Hammond continued with his tinkering and inventing, which became ever more involved with the supernatural.

One of his experiments, for instance, included a large wooden cage that purportedly helped to determine if psychics really held mystical powers or not, according to Thomas D'Agostino in *Haunted Massachusetts*. Bulky and dangerous—it was said to burn holes in the floor—it was used to block current; mediums were deemed "real" if they could pick up on the pulse from the next world without extemporaneous energy contaminating it. Hammond also held regular séances and kept a number of cats—long revered, from the ancient Chinese to the Egyptians, for their metaphysical attributes—and often proclaimed his wishes to be reincarnated as one.

Hammond was also known for his idiosyncratic attributes and morbid antics.

Unlike many of us, he didn't shy away at all from the notion of death. He occasionally lunched on the roof of an Aztec-like tomb he had built for himself on his estate, according to Cheri Revai in *Haunted Massachusetts: Ghosts and Strange Phenomena of the Bay State*, and he was known to ask visitors if they'd like to see where he would be buried.

Purportedly, the inside doors of his tomb are outfitted with locks, and Hammond also stipulated in his will that poison ivy be planted around his grave—clearly, in death, just as in life, he deigned to come and go as he pleased— and be unperturbed in doing so.

Just as at ease with nudity, he was known to frequently swim naked. He also commissioned an anatomically correct statue of himself—his wife, mortified, hired a sculptor to conceal the statue's genitals with a fig leaf.

Terrorizing visitors was another pastime; in one of the guest rooms, he had a doorway layered over with wallpaper, so that, when closed, it was indistinguishable from the adjoining walls. In the middle of the night, aided by one of his many remote controls, the sly inventor liked to close the door—so that guests, upon awakening, would be frantic and trapped.

And his antics didn't stop when he—or at least his earthly form—did. After his death in 1965 at age seventy-seven, visitors and staff alike reported strange echoes and the squeak of soft-soled shoes on stone floors (perhaps Hammond sneaking up on them or plotting his next prank). Irene, for her part, has been seen peering out of castle windows.

Stray cats, as they did during Hammond's lifetime, continue to wander without hesitation into the castle and take up residence. In one of the well-circulated stories, not long after the proprietor's death, a large black cat was seen sauntering in, navigating its passages as if it were already intimately familiar with them. It then bounded up and nestled into one of Hammond's favorite chairs.

Those who knew him were said to be nonplussed—how could they be? It would stand to reason that Hammond would be just as curious a character in death as he was in life.

Chapter 20

The Restless Ephraim Gray

The workmen, tasked with disinterring and reburying bodies in Malden's oldest cemetery to make way for city expansion, were making substantial progress.

When they arrived at an 1850 tomb marked "Gray," they cracked it open and cleaned out the dirt and debris hefted from the coffin.

And they found it to be unusually light.

Interests piqued, they used a crowbar to jostle its hinges apart, the accumulated dust and grime of centuries temporarily clouding the air.

They were baffled. It was empty.

But in the case of Ephraim Gray, a notorious recluse and concocter of potions, the discovery—or, more accurately, lack thereof—was hardly confounding. The wealthy, mid-nineteenth-century hermit had been obsessed with extending his life beyond earthly—and bodily—confines.

In the 1800s, Gray lived in a house as creaky and temperamental as he was in the center of Malden, just outside Boston and originally part of the hub's oldest neighborhood Charlestown. A chemist, lifelong bachelor, and secretive hermit, he was moody, crotchety, taciturn. Never entertaining friends or visitors, his only companion was a faithful, quiet, and unquestioning male servant.

But those who wish to be left alone often incite the most curiosity; many of the city's nosy busybodies gossiped about the goings-on in the scientist's mysterious manor. It was said that a repulsive, overpowering odor of chemicals permeated the house and grounds, even causing some passersby to gag. The odd and recondite old man was believed to dedicate all his efforts, day and night, to developing a youthful elixir, and some say he ingested a strange potion every day.

The overly curious and brave trespassed on his property, sneaking up and peeping into his smudged and filthy windows. Fertile imaginations propagated stories of shadows inside that appeared like goblins.

His eccentric and alchemistic practices continued until his death in 1850—when things got even more bizarre.

On his deathbed, he reportedly said to his unflagging servant (whose name has not been recorded, perhaps known only to his master), "In my life, I have differed from other men, and by the foul fiend I will continue different after I am dead. My flesh is not common flesh, like yours. It will never rot."

After his final (recorded) breath, he had one last vexing request. As relayed by his servant, he asked that his body be interred completely undisturbed and untouched— no autopsy, no embalming, no removal of fluids. The flummoxed coroner balked but ultimately kept Ephraim Gray's final wish.

He was soon buried, his estate doled out, his silent attendant free to finish out his own days in obscurity.

But curiosity is one of life's few true immortalities; as the years passed, his perplexing story continued to linger and intrigue.

Not twenty years later, a group of Harvard medical students were musing over Gray's strange story. One night, on impulse (and perhaps fueled by the inherent spontaneity of wine) they climbed into a carriage and rode to nearby Malden. Creeping into the cemetery in the middle of the city, they located Gray's tomb around midnight and pushed open the heavy, ornate iron door.

With a chisel, they pried open his coffin, creaked back the heavy lid, and held their lanterns aloft for a glimpse.

Astonished, the old man looked like he was merely sleeping, not at all decayed, cheeks still flush with the color of life (although his clothes were slowly deteriorating around his slim shape).

Not wishing to further disturb his slumber, they carefully replaced the lid, put the coffin back in its place, then returned to Cambridge—where it was said they dedicated significant time to reproducing his mystical elixir.

Another of their classmates, upon hearing of their late-night exploits, set out on a more desecrating mission. Taking his own carriage to the cemetery, camouflaged by the dark night and equipped with sharp tools, he entered the notorious crypt alone.

His intention: to saw off Gray's head and return with it to his lab, where he could take the time to give it a full examination.

He set to the grisly work, laboriously carving through skin, ligaments, and bone. But just as he had completely severed the head, holding it up for closer inspection, Gray apparently expressed his irate displeasure in the defilement.

Ghoulish whispers emanated from the darkest corners of the tomb; moans, wails, and shrieks grew closer, filling his ears; footsteps trod outside on the wet grass. When the medical student saw what he believed were shadows taking ghoulish form and descending upon him, he threw the disembodied head on the cold crypt floor and fled the burial ground.

Thirty years later, when the dead were displaced to make way for progress in the way of an expanded road through the city—as which, we have read, has happened many a time in the cramped areas of New England settled by our forefathers—Gray's casket was discovered empty.

And his remains, it should be noted, were never found. So perhaps the esoteric alchemist did ultimately uncover the secret to eternal life—keeping, as was his way, one of the enduring questions befuddling and stumping humankind greedily, furtively, to himself.

Chapter 21
The Lure of the Grave

Frankenstein, Mary Shelley's tormented tale of madness, obsession, love, and the sinister perils of flouting natural order through necromancy, has haunted for centuries.

But what many may not know is that the English Romantic poet and novelist—whose love life was said to be as tumultuous as those of the characters she wrote about—based at least part of her macabre novel on the very real custom of grave robbing. A morbid, desecrating tradition as old as burial itself, it was believed to have been practiced both on distant shores and in the burgeoning American colonies as medicine was evolving and doctors were in need of fresh bodies for experimenting their craft.

One such location that was said to condone the grisly practice—and spawned at least one lovelorn urban legend—was Cambridge's Holden Chapel, according to paranormal researcher Sam Baltrusis.

A squat brick building in Harvard Yard with an intricately engraved front gable, it was built in 1744, serving as both a religious gathering place and a lecture hall for Harvard students (and not long after, as was the case with many a local buildings during the Revolutionary War, a rooming house for patriot soldiers).

Later, it became Harvard's first cadaver room and also a location for professors and students to hold anatomy and physiology dissections.

But at the time, with today's common practice of organ donation still decades away, fresh, dead bodies were often difficult to come by—thus necessitating the ancient tradition of removing the newly dead from their resting places.

The practice went like this: Resurrection men (as is the case with many who perform the dreckish duties of society, grave robbers attempted to inflate their perverse sentries with a glorified title) kept close records of local deaths, including how and when they met their demise, their ages, injuries, and when and where they were buried. Then, when the opportunity arose, they slunk into the graveyard, removed the recently interred bodies, and made quick money by selling the bodies to medical schools—often with no questions asked.

One rumored grave robber was Harvard janitor Ephraim Littlefield, according to Baltrusis, who was purportedly sent out to retrieve fresh cadavers when the school's stock was dwindling. (If true, Littlefield later redeemed himself when he helped to solve the notorious murder of wealthy Bostonian Dr. George Parkman, as we will read further on.)

At least one aggrieved spirit is said to make her dissatisfaction with the defiling practice eternally known.

On a frigid early-winter night in the 1800s, when the building was still a cadaver room, a beautiful young woman with the surname Pickham was said to be riding nearby in a sleigh with her fiancé. Horses, much as their four-wheeled successors, were just as prone to black ice; the one guiding the young couple's sled was said to suddenly slip, flipping its riders. The hysterical bride-to-be discovered her lover with his neck broken; he died in her arms as she wailed. He was soon laid to rest at the nearby Old Burial Ground—but it was believed that his young body, a fresh cadaver for experimentation, was quickly dug up and sold, according to Baltrusis.

The heartbroken young woman never recovered, and she became convinced that her lover's body had been sneaked away to the dissection lab. As the story goes, she was said to escape the confines of her nearby family home every year as the first snow fell, pounding on the door of the laboratory until she was dragged away, sobbing and exhausted, by family members.

To this day, a female spirit is said to appear around the year's first snowstorm, bewailing her lover's fate—yet never leaving footprints of her deplorable passage.

And perhaps there is truth to her eternal lament: When the chapel was renovated in 1999, according to Baltrusis, archaeologists unearthed human remains in its basement—including sawed-up skeletons—alongside the expected detritus of scientific experiments, such as broken glassware and test tubes.

Only the spirits themselves—who have no voices—can say what sacrifices they made for the betterment of science.

Nearby, the 1759 Christ Church Cambridge, the city's oldest, boasts spooks of its own.

Long scorned by locals because of its Tory leanings—Tories were loyalists to the British crown, and the rectory was built by members of the Church of England who lived in the area deemed "Tory Row"—it was attacked by patriots during the Revolution (even though both Americans and British worshiped there). Sitting adjacent to it in Harvard Square is Cambridge's Old Burial Ground. Established before 1635, according to the city, it serves as the final resting place of a wide array of people—from nameless paupers to well-regarded presidents of Harvard University, to felled redcoats—and is spotted with 1,218 gravestones (but believed to hold far more dead than that).

Buried within its elaborate subterranean John Vassal tomb—last opened in 1862, according to the city, and replete with twenty-five caskets—is Lt. Richard Brown, a redcoat who was shot down in the street in 1778, according to Baltrusis. After losing control of his horse-drawn carriage, he was stopped by a patriot watchman; when Brown pointed to his sword, which indicated his rank and privilege, he was shot point-blank in the head. That year, he was interred in the Vassal tomb, a move that so enraged local colonists that they ransacked Christ Church.

Brown also allegedly expresses his eternal displeasure. It is said that he audibly shuffles throughout the church, tempestuously slamming doors or snuffing out candles.

Beyond its ostensible haunting, the church, like many buildings in and around Boston, has a significant and storied history. It once hosted George and Martha Washington, who took part in a rally to keep the building from falling into disrepair, as well as Teddy Roosevelt, who was a Sunday school teacher while studying at Harvard University, and Benjamin Spock and Martin Luther King Jr., who both announced their opposition to the controversial Vietnam War.

Maybe, in addition to his anger over his rash death at the barrel of a bellicose patriot's gun, Brown keeps his enduring vigil at the church so as to not be forgotten among such luminaries (whether sharing his Tory sentiments or not).

Chapter 22

Eternally Disturbed

Trudge up a steep, uneven hill, graves of slate and limestone all around lilting forward and backward, left and right, battling with gravity, to a middling-sized mausoleum identified with "Pierce." Further marked with the year 1883 and a simple cross, it is a modest resting place bordered with concrete pilings, an earthen mound at its back covered with patchy grass and sporadic strings of ivy.

But inspect it a little closer and this pyramid-shaped tomb with its subtle Christian iconography seems a little too reinforced for such a bucolic graveyard built into a steep slope in the center of historic Newburyport.

Its front and back are completely bricked up and further fortified with layers of thick mortar, and there are no identifying additional markings, dates, or names as to who sleeps within.

In other words—no way in, no way out.

Some so-called resting places, for whatever reason, simply attract the sinister. Such is the case with this inauspicious grave in the Old Hill Burying Ground, containing the remains of several members of the Pierce family of Newburyport, who died of numerous causes—including drowning and tuberculosis—between 1863 and 1899, as noted by Roxie Zwicker in *Massachusetts Book of the Dead: Graveyard Legends and Lore.*

Over the last ninety years, the family mausoleum has been desecrated three times. As a result, its eternal residents are said to be restless; willowy figures have reportedly been seen passing through the door of the tomb and crossing the burial ground. Paranormal researchers claim to have captured infrared images of their forms and their laborious passage across the grounds, as well as unexplained heads jutting from the ground nearby.

Vandals first disturbed the tomb in 1925, gaining entrance by digging an opening at the back of it and breaking in through crumbled stonework, according to Zwicker. Once inside, they yanked the coffins open, ripped the clothing from the decaying skeletons, then danced around in the rotting nineteenth-century garb. The bodies were also accosted; wrenched from their coffins, their deteriorating forms were manipulated into seated positions and poked with sticks.

The defilers were reported and confessed, the bodies then replaced, the tomb resealed.

Sixty years passed, but the Pierces could not ultimately rest easy. In 1985, looters struck again; gaining entrance, three young men created a macabre clubhouse of sorts in the tomb. Drinking themselves, they egregiously dumped alcohol into the corpses' mouths. Again, clothing was removed from the bodies, and this time, the vandals took souvenirs of the silver nameplates that marked the bodies. According to Zwicker, after a caretaker discovered the offense, a front-page plea in the local newspaper drew the trio forward, and they were examined for disease after their long nights of exposure to the dead bodies.

And the desecration continued. In 2005, a young man doing court-ordered community service in the cemetery for a burglary conviction booted the Pierce tomb open once again. Brutally twisting off one of the skeleton's spine, collarbone, and skull, he posed for pictures with it, according to the Associated Press, then kicked it around like a soccer ball (it was discovered in a hole several feet away). He was eventually charged with two felonies, and police lieutenant Richard Siemasko expressed the bewildered sentiment held by many at the time.

"It's bizarre, absolutely bizarre," he told the Associated Press. "This is just a whole new level of weird for me."

The tomb has since been resealed—perpetually, this time?—so perhaps now the long-besieged family can finally appreciate their long-overdue slumber.

Chapter 23

More Aggrieved Dead

ARE SOULS MERELY A HUMAN PHENOMENON?

As the story goes, in the 1600s, a marvelous tree stood greeting the *Mayflower* passengers in an area they would soon parcel off and name "Duxbury." A suburb of Boston, the small town was traversed by the Bay Path (or the historic Boston Post Road), and the oak's advantageous placement eventually made it a prime spot, prior to the establishment of the postal service, for independent runners to pick up and leave messages and packages for townspeople.

Once more sophisticated forms of mail delivery emerged in the late 1700s, residents nailed a box to the fabled old tree—what some consider America's first postal box—and it became known throughout town as the "Tree of Knowledge" as mail was passed back and forth for decades under its broad branches.

By the mid-nineteenth century, however, the box fell into disuse, and the tree was neglected and forgotten. In 1845, townspeople barely noticed when it was felled in a tremendous storm.

And it would have been left to rot—had not an elderly patriarch told his fellow resident of an alarming vision. In a dream, the spirit of the old oak chided him and the town for failing to recognize its role in the success of the community, then prophesied that if the spot where it stood were to remain unmarked, Duxbury would be forever cursed.

Wary of such omens, the townspeople set up a wooden plaque commemorating the tree; over the years, more permanent monuments erected, and today, the fabled old oak is recalled with a granite barrier that "should eternally protect Duxbury citizens from misfortune and disaster."

It's a story lending credence to the fact that more than humans may bear souls.

MEASURING THE SOUL?

In 1906, Duncan MacDougall, a doctor at Massachusetts General Hospital, set out to offer proof that the human soul indeed has a substance. To support his case, he created a device consisting of a bed frame layered over a system of finely calibrated scales (said to measure weight to the tenth of an ounce). He then sought volunteers who were expiring (those with tuberculosis were particularly good candidates). As they were dying, he laid them on his contraption. In every case—after taking into account substance loss such as air from the lungs and urinary and fecal matter—he was said to determine that the body, at the instant of death, lost several measurable ounces.

So perhaps there is truth to the concept of a weighty soul.

MEANWHILE, ON TO A MEATIER MATTER . . .

Reading this any further requires a thick skin.

Nothing is quite as grotesque as the notion of human flesh being used as anything but. Of course, over the millennia—spanning the reigns of many monarchs and dictators, conquerors and combatants—human beings have been horrifically creative in their methods of torturing and disfiguring one another, including, when it comes to the precious flesh: flaying, excoriating, searing, scalping, and tanning.

Then there was the practice of what's termed anthropodermic bibliopegy—or binding books in human skin. Yes, it might sound like something straight out of a Clive Barker story, but it was a real custom—if nowhere near approaching even the darkest, dustiest far-reaching corner of the shadow cast by mainstream culture. Although the details aren't exactly, shall we say, fleshed out, it was said to originate, like many abominable rituals, in the Middle Ages. The first alleged instance was said to be a French Bible from the 1200s, according to experts, while other supposed flesh-bound volumes are believed to date to the sixteenth and seventeenth centuries.

Bibliophiles—and dermaphiliacs, or those with an attraction to skin—can literally press the flesh with a handful of local flesh-bound volumes. One of the city's most infamous resides at the Boston Athenaeum, a two-hundred-year-old membership library, sections of which are open to visitors and tours. Within its stacks of roughly half a million tomes—according to the Athenaeum website—is the memoir of serial robber and thief James Allen. *Hic Liber Waltonis Cute Compactus Est*, or *The Highwayman: Narrative of the Life of James Allen alias George Walton*, a literally skin-deep autobiography, was supposedly made at the criminal's own request and presented upon his death to a man who once resisted Allen's attempts to rob him.

Meanwhile, in the Houghton Library at nearby Harvard University, *Des destinées de l'ame* is said to have been crafted from a section of epidermis from the back of an unclaimed female mental patient who died of a stroke, according to the library. Containing a collection of essays on the soul and life after death by French writer Arsène Houssaye, it was a gift to his friend Dr. Ludovic Bouland. Gold trimmed and hued greenish gold, it was "bound in human skin parchment on which no ornament has been stamped to preserve its elegance," Bouland penned in a note accompanying the manuscript, according to the well-regarded school newspaper, the *Harvard Crimson*.

"By looking carefully you easily distinguish the pores of the skin. A book about the human soul deserved to have a human covering." (Whatever you say, Doctor. . . .)

In June 2014, the school announced that a rare book conservator was "99.9 percent confident" that the binding was of human origin—a deduction that came about after research of microscopic samples and peptide mass fingerprinting, a protein-identification process.

Similarly, Harvard's Countway Library of Medicine is said to house a sixteenth-century French translation of Roman poet Ovid's *Metamorphoses*, according to the *Crimson*, and the school's Langdell Law Library, meanwhile, holds the 1605 Spanish law book *Practicarum quaestionum circa leges regias* (both volumes purportedly flesh-bound).

The final page of the latter describes the alleged fate of its man-made encasement, Jonas Wright, who was "flayed alive" in August 1632, the book being one of the poor man's chief possessions, "together with ample of his skin to bynd it." (However, the school has since debunked that statement through scientific testing, determining that it is, in fact, encased in sheep hide. However—if a droll pun can be employed—it makes for quite the skin-crawling story.)

An eighty-three-year-old article from the university's school newspaper also made note of a 1933 exhibit on miniature books that included *Little Poems for Little Folk*, bound from twenty square inches of the skin of a donor's back.

Talk about spine-tingling tales.

THE UNREST OF A FOUNDING FATHER

For centuries, locals had long pondered the final resting place of Myles Standish, a *Mayflower* passenger and dignitary who was instrumental in the founding of the earliest colonies.

According to court documents, he was believed to have died in October 1656, and local tradition had it that his burial place was marked by "peculiar" three-cornered stones lying due east and west about six feet apart in the town's disused and neglected old cemetery, according to the 1914 account, *The Graves of Myles Standish and Other Pilgrims*, by E. J. V. Huiginn.

In Huiginn's retelling, town selectmen gave permission in 1891 for the grave to be opened. When the excavators hit upon the coffin, they diligently set down their tools and carefully used their hands and smaller digging instruments to dislodge it.

Inside, they found a skeleton in a "wonderful state of preservation," measuring five feet seven inches, with a large and broad skull and bones that indicated "a man of tremendous physique and strength," according to Huiginn. Beside him they discovered the bodies of two women, determined to be his daughter Lora Standish and his daughter-in-law Mary Standish, based on his will.

"We all felt unusually quiet and even solemn," Huiginn wrote. "Here were the remains of the man who had done so much for Plymouth Colony and consequently for all of us."

The remains were reburied, a memorial was soon erected—today marked with a large buttress, stone, sign, cannons, and cannonballs.

Townspeople and historians alike, as well as Standish himself, could finally rest easy.

Part 7

RESTLESS SPIRITS

They are the restive ones, the wanderers—lost, purposeless (or decidedly purposeful), unavenged, unappeased, morose, heartbroken. For whatever reason—revenge, missed opportunities, lost contact, indifference, indecision—their ghostly specters remain among us.

Chapter 24

Where the Party Never Ends

Multicolored, varying in size, the nebulous streaks of light dart, flit, and linger; pulse, zigzag, and whirl; pirouette, spiral, and undulate around the dusky studio.

It's not until after the pole-dancing instructor, clad in a tube top, miniskirt, and thigh-high boots, watches a video of herself spinning, twirling, and pivoting that she actually gets a look at the mysterious entities—and realizes that they appear to be moving in sync with her.

Wendy Reardon of Gypsy Rose Dancing isn't sure, but she believes that at least some of these sentient orbs that regularly manifest around her as she practices her moves emanated from the site of the tragic Cocoanut Grove nightclub fire (which used to be just paces from her one-time Boylston Street studio).

"They've got some kind of intelligence," she told Sam Baltrusis, author of *Ghosts of Boston: Haunts of the Hub*, "because they'll swirl around, under, over, and sometimes they'll even hover."

Although they were consumed in the catastrophic 1942 conflagration of the once-renowned post-Prohibition Boston lounge—the deadliest-known nightclub fire in the world— some Cocoanut Grove patrons may dance still.

And others, no doubt stunned for eternity by the intensity and rapidity of the blaze, are believed to loiter and listlessly roam in other ways, as well.

HISTORY IGNITES

It was a little after 10:15 p.m. Down on Piedmont Street, at the edge of Boston's theater district, the Cocoanut Grove was boisterous.

Locals, visitors, and luminaries were crammed into the legendary nightclub's bar, two lounges, and dining room—some lining up outside in the brisk late-fall air for a half hour or more before being granted entrance. They sipped fifty-cent mixed drinks; danced the Lindy Hop and the rumba; listened to swing music and rollicking pianos while enjoying two-dollar steak dinners in the Grove's tropical-themed atmosphere of overarching artificial palm trees, blue satin ceilings, imitation leather walls, and zebra-striped furniture.

It was November 28. The Saturday after Thanksgiving. A weekend of celebrations and homecomings. (As well as the night Worcester's College of the Holy Cross unexpectedly routed Boston College, 55–12 in a highly anticipated football game held at Fenway Park.) A time of respite to temporarily dismiss thoughts of the dominating war.

Suddenly, in the basement's Melody Lounge, above the cacophony of music and voices: shouts—initially inaudible, but judging by the tone, clearly frantic.

Heads turned. Shoulders, elbows, and hips jabbed into each other, toes tromping on other toes, in a space overly crowded with bodies. Dancers and diners shared quizzical looks of concern.

What was going on?

Within seconds, it was clear—and for many, it was also far too late.

An overwhelming whoosh transformed the windowless space into a momentary vacuum, sucking up all sound.

Voracious flames, flicking a scorching blue, yellow, and white, broiled in waves across the ceiling of the basement lounge.

Panic. Terror. Chaos. A tangle of bodies running, stumbling, tumbling, crawling, clambering over each other, hands grabbing and clawing; curses, screams of pain and fear. Pops and explosions as fake trees, tables, chairs, fabric, wood, and glass were engulfed. Strobing darkness and light as the electricity was quickly extinguished. The overpowering smell of gases and smoke made acrid as both the natural and unnatural caught flame.

Within just two minutes, the ball of fire was racing up the stairs to the main floor. There, dancers crowded on the parquet dance area and diners clustered at cramped tables—as many, it was said, as could be filled in the space to accommodate an increased number of guests for a busy holiday weekend.

On her way back from dancing, survivor Louise Bouvier described suddenly seeing "a flash, a black curtain," then falling unconscious after taking a breath of "hot, gassy air."

Medical student Joseph Dreyfus, eating with friends in the nearby dining area, also remembered a "sheet of flame." "It was very hot, and I put my hands up to my face, which saved my eyes," he said, "and the next thing I knew I was on the floor." (Dreyfus, who later became a surgeon, lost his wife in the blaze. And for the rest of his life, he was plagued by the skin grafts on his injured hands; as a gruesome reminder of the deadly night, whenever he scrubbed for an operation, he noted, "my gloves were full of blood.")

In just five minutes, the entire building was overwhelmed with flames and smoke, which surged in orange veins and nasty ebony clouds through any open cracks and crevasses into the night sky. Alarmed drivers in the area, seeing the inferno, abandoned their cars, choking the cobblestone streets and blocking the way of first responders.

"It seemed like the building behind us . . . was bursting," recalled Mary Barbara Brennan Dannaher, a patron who was lucky enough to leave before the fire erupted, but doubled back after news of the pyre spread through the surrounding area nearly as quickly as the lashing flames absorbed the two-level brick structure.

Many inside—particularly in the basement—simply had no chance; they were asphyxiated or burned alive in a blistering tomb. Those who could escape did so out Cocoanut's revolving front door—but adding to the pandemonium, it soon became jammed by pressure from both inside and outside, with the helpless victims within beating at it with frenetic fists.

"You could hear them and you could see them," Thomas I. Gray, a Navy officer who was in the area and rushed to the site to help out with relief efforts, said of the trapped, doomed souls.

Others were able to save themselves by jumping out of windows or prying open exit doors that were either concealed or not known to the majority of patrons; some successfully hid from the devouring flare-up in refrigerators and meat lockers, and others were said to protect their mouth and lungs with makeshift masks of urine-soaked kerchiefs and large ice-cream containers.

Gray recalled the depravity evident in the aftermath. Many who had managed to slip out to safety had had their "shirts torn off," he recalled, and their backs were "bloody from where people had clawed them just like wild animals."

The discord of police sirens and fire alarms cleaved the chilly night. Firemen quickly set to quenching the inferno with increasingly frigid water that froze on the sidewalk as the temperature dropped. Once doused, the area around the building was a mass of locals, policemen, firemen, reporters, and family members who set to work hoisting ladders, passing stretchers hand-over-hand, and hefting victims—both the limp dead as well as the living (delirious, disheveled, eyebrows singed and faces smudged with soot).

Inside, the revolting stench of scorching flesh intermingled with the bitterly pungent smoke. Bodies were found in all states—charred, trampled, piled on top of one another, collapsed, or simply seated in their chairs, unable to react before the fire had overtaken them. More and more bodies were laid out on the street and enshrouded, awaiting identification. Survivors were transported to nearby hospitals, where some later perished and others underwent life-saving and cosmetic procedures.

All told, 492 were killed—including Western movie star Buck Jones, who was in the area while on a national war bond campaign tour—another 166 were injured, and the circa-1927 building's nearly 10,000 square feet was destroyed in a matter of moments. Inside, the once-beloved nightclub, with its multiple bars, ballroom, bandstand, and dining room with a ceiling that could be retracted on warm, starry nights, was a ruin of destruction—walls charred and singed, hallways gutted, ceiling and floor bulging and heaving, once majestic rooms a disarray of heaped-up chairs and tables, floors littered with the detritus of revelry—mini drink umbrellas, cups, plates, overturned platters.

A quickly ensuing investigation found that the night club had been crammed with nearly 1,000 people—roughly double its legal capacity. Victim Bouvier attested to this in her statement, calling it "very crowded, mobbed—mobbed."

Likewise, doors that could have served as escape routes were found to be either locked or inaccessible. A series of hearings, inquests, and indictments (handed to various officials, the building's interior designer, construction contractor, and construction foreman) soon followed. Club owner Barney Welansky was found guilty of nineteen counts of manslaughter and was sentenced to twelve to fifteen years in prison (although he only served three).

Ultimately, the source of the violent, deadly fire was never definitively determined—although many theories have been floated over the years, from the spark of an unassuming match lit by a young busboy, to faulty electrical wiring, to a mix of toxic gases, or combustible ceiling tile adhesive.

But as with all things, time moved on. The legendary (and now infamous) Cocoanut Grove was demolished less than three years later, in September 1945, the area where it once entertained so many partygoers overtaken by a paved parking lot adjacent to the Boston Radisson Hotel and theater complex. The only memorial is a small plaque, set into the brick sidewalk, featuring the Grove's floor plan (complete with its festive coconut trees) and stating "Phoenix out of the Ashes."

BURNED INTO TIME

Still, even as the smoke cleared, memories—and, it's said, some spirits—linger.

Shadowy victims, discombobulated, dressed in clothes torn and bitten away by fire, have been seen wandering around the site, as well as the halls of the Radisson, hastily appearing and just as soon disappearing, wispy and willowy as the smoke that obscured that night. Perhaps they perpetually seek out a path to safety, or search for a loved one forever lost to them among the smoke and flames.

Workers and visitors to the hotel bar and kitchen have also reported strange noises, flashes, and popping sounds.

In what seem to be spectral instances of overcompensation, meanwhile, the Stuart Street Playhouse near the site has experienced numerous instances of flooding throughout the building that some say seems far too pervasive to be random. Employees have also been said to discover auditorium seats completely soaked—with absolutely no explanation (such as an expected leak from above).

More macabre visions have occurred at other locales. One nearby building, now the site of the drag lounge Jacques Cabaret, served as a temporary morgue on that devastating night in 1942; bodies were carried down and lined in rows. In one story, a former bartender, when cleaning up late one night, was jolted when he suddenly saw several bodies lying across the floor of the darkened bar area. As soon as he turned on the light, they were gone.

But spirits can be playful, as well—as Wendy Reardon has purportedly discovered.

The dancing instructor first noticed distinctive orbs moving with and around her as she was taping her routines in her studio in Quincy, Massachusetts, just south of Boston; when viewed later, the curious white and blue shapes appeared receptive to her struts and twists, coordinating with her as she maneuvered around the pole. Over time, as she has honed her moves for the camera, she has continued to videotape the beings—sometimes even capturing them darting and whizzing in her peripheral vision.

When she relocated to Boylston Street, just a short walk from the former Cocoanut Grove site on adjacent Piedmont

Street, they seemed to decidedly increase in number. Now she claims to have multiple otherworldly dancing partners that she playfully names based on their distinctive qualities—"Bullet," who moves like one, for example, or "Blinky," who flickers in and out like a firefly.

"I like to think some of them are those spirits [from Cocoanut Grove] finishing their night out," Reardon, also an author and a papal scholar who claims to have discovered the gift of mediumship six years ago, told the British website Caters News Agency. She believes that the entities—whoever or whatever they are—came upon her dancing one day, were attracted to her energy, "and so they told their ghost friends to come, too."

When walking around the former site, meanwhile, she's witnessed some similarly unique phenomena. During one stop on a twilit evening, for example, she discovered a long lacy black glove—torn and dusty, bereft of its mate—near the memorial plaque. As she held it in her hand to video, she caught what she identified as four different orbs circulating, the most marked of which appears sooty and flies up along the length of the glove.

"I actually got chills when I picked it up," she said of discovering the garment, although she acknowledged that she's not sure whether it was indeed a remnant, phantom or not, of that tragic night. "I was going to take it with me but definitely got the feeling to leave it there."

Overall, she described a sense of deep melancholy and loneliness emanating from the site. "I literally have to tear myself away when I leave," she said, describing a distinct feeling of "people not wanting me to leave, to stay and hold their hands."

Victims, perhaps, seeking a guide out of the darkness that engulfed them and so many others on that fateful night.

Chapter 25

Gloucester's Ghost Ship

An early-spring night out on the ocean. The midnight moon shimmers on the lightly dancing current of the Atlantic. The sky is scattered with the ghosts of stars. It is quiet but for the faint splashing nudges of water as the fishing schooner drifts lackadaisically on the waves.

Commissioned out of Gloucester, the *Charles Haskell* has been out to sea for what was several days of bounteous fishing.

Below, the crew sleeps. Above, two sentinels watch out over the water, bantering, smoking, dozing, sitting for long periods of silence with their thoughts.

Suddenly, jarring the calm: a strange, subtle thumping sound on one side of the boat. Followed by another.

Almost as if . . .

And then the colorless, water-bloated hands begin to reach over the ship's side rails.

Ghastly figures haul themselves up and over the *Haskell's* side. Ruinous corpses emerge on deck—eye sockets left empty and gaping by nibbling fish; tattered oilskin, deteriorated and bitten away by the salty brew of the water, barely clinging to bony, wasted frames; soggy hair matted against expressionless faces; boots tracing a squishy-suction with their shambling movements.

Roughly two dozen in all, they pay no heed to the shocked and horrified sentries. Moving out of a regimented routine, they rig sails, set anchor, and take up positions on benches around the deck, casting invisible lines out into the water from which they mysteriously materialized.

And, as word gets around the ship of the ghoulish crew that had come aboard, drawing the astonished and terrified human fishermen—captain included—out of their bunks and into the crisp night air, that's how they remain.

Finally, when dawn breaks, the first hints of daylight casting both the living and inanimate objects in subtly coalescing silhouettes, the ghostly crew unmans their stations, then drops, one by one, back into the sea.

Bringing its own unique flourish to the term "ghost ship," the haunting episode spells the end of the short—but ill-fated—career of the *Haskell*.

Built in 1869 for cod fishing off the Massachusetts coast, the schooner was considered by many as doomed from the very start. During its initial inspection that spring, a workman slipped and broke his neck. With seafarers superstitious by nature, a death before the ship even left port was a terrible omen; as a result, the would-be captain refused to set sail. With such a harbinger of bad tidings deterring many potential captains and crewmen, it took a year for anyone willful and brave enough—and not leery of such ill premonitions—to volunteer to sail her. After the ship sat idle for months, that someone happened to be Capt. Clifford Curtis of Gloucester.

With a crew of sixteen men, he soon set out in the midst of winter on the *Haskell*'s disastrous maiden voyage. The destination: Georges Bank, a large and plentiful fishing ground that spans from Cape Cod in Massachusetts all the way up to Nova Scotia. In the winter of 1869–1870, many vessels were in the area catching cod and halibut, and the *Haskell* dropped anchor among them.

Soon, the atmosphere turned foreboding; the *Haskell* was not done with her vile ways. The sky brewed into a dark mass, the ocean boiled, the wind tossed and tumbled boats like baubles. As a treacherous hurricane descended, Captain Curtis ordered his anchor lines to be cut. This quick and decisive action freed the ship from its tether that was tumultuously knocking it up, down, and around, ultimately sparing it irremediable damage.

However, it affirmed utter disaster for another nearby schooner. The tactical maneuver set the *Haskell* on a direct collision course with the Salem sloop the *Andrew Johnson*. Unable to direct or divert itself in the midst of violent, over-powering waves and wind, the Gloucester ship rammed the *Andrew Johnson* into oblivion, effectively slicing it in half, rapidly sinking it, and sending its crew, with no time to react, to horrid drowning deaths. (Accounts vary of the number of men lost; some say ten, others as many as twenty-six.)

Shaken but relieved that their lives were spared, the *Haskell* crew performed stopgap repairs as their ship diverted back to port for an overhaul.

Not one to be deterred or lend credence to premonitions, Captain Curtis had the ship back at Georges Bank within a few months, just as soon as it was seaworthy. The spring of 1870 was much less stormy, and the crew had a few robust days of fishing—until that fateful midnight watch.

As the literal skeleton crew abruptly overtook the *Haskell* and just as quickly absconded, Curtis was finally spooked. He and his men believed that these were the vengeful spirits of the crew of the *Andrew Johnson*, who had met their cold, lonely deaths in the frigid, turbulent, unforgiving waters of the Atlantic.

As the apparitions disappeared with the dawn, the captain ordered the boat turned back toward Gloucester Harbor. His men readily obeyed.

But with the coast more than a day's sail away, they were prepared for another harrowing night dominated by the specters of the men they had watched drown.

And the following evening, again around the bewitching hour, the phantoms returned; they slung their rotting bodies up onto the deck and silently went about their duties. The human seamen watched, both helpless and enraptured, until again dawn began to reach its tendrils across the dark night. This time, when they departed with the beckoning far-off shore in sight, they climbed overboard and walked silently atop the water in the direction of their home, Salem, before vanishing from mortal sight.

The *Haskell* soon returned to harbor, and it was said she never again sailed the open sea. Because of her untoward history, she was shunned, and her exact fate is unknown. Some say she was forgotten, left to fester and disintegrate into the depths of the Gloucester harbor; others say she was bought by a Canadian captain who never ultimately set her on the water again.

As for the crew of the *Andrew Johnson*? They may yet haunt the Atlantic shores, restless from their early demise, obediently fulfilling their sworn oaths as fishermen for all time.

Chapter 26

The Long and Winding Road

They call him the "storm breeder." His is a story of how obstinacy and ego can ricochet and backfire, ultimately leading to ruination and—we can only assume, as his apparition only repeats the same questions and entreaties over and over—eternal regret. Some take the story of the roaming Peter Rugg as pure folklore; others consider him to be one of Boston's oldest ghosts, damned and lost for all time.

In 1770, as colonial sentiment was being inflamed against the British occupiers by such bloody provocations as the Boston Massacre, Peter Rugg was a wealthy merchant, overseeing and peddling stables and pastures of horses and cattle. Living on Middle Street in South Boston with his wife Catharine and young daughter, he was successful, forthright, respected, and "generally esteemed for his sober life and manners," William Austin wrote in an 1824 story (which many say is fictionalized) of Rugg, subtitled "The Missing Man."

But he was also notorious for his blustery and proud demeanor. As Austin described, when the infirmity of his temper was roused, he was "altogether ungovernable, his language 'profane' and 'terrible.'" He was known to kick his way through doors, literally somersault with fury, so vigorous in his raving that he could bite nails in half and send his wig (which was the customary costume of men and boys of the day) flying straight off his head.

"While these fits were on him," Austin wrote, he had "no respect for heaven or earth." But otherwise, he was a "good sort of man," and "nobody was so ready to commend a placid temper."

One morning he set out for a business trip to nearby Concord—roughly twenty miles west and very shortly to become renowned for its role as the opening theater of the war (to which Rugg would remain forever ignorant). He harnessed his carriage and black steed, ignoring the portents of an impending storm. At her behest, he brought his ten-year-old daughter, Jenny, along for what he believed would be a quick day trip to the pastoral countryside.

They passed beyond the cramped confines of Boston, Rugg saw to his business in town, and the father and daughter set off for the return trip. But as forecast, the sky grew dark and threatening, hazy, then gray, then black with tormented thunder clouds. The storm struck; pummeling rain, wicked winds, cacophonous thunder.

Stopping as soon as was feasible, Rugg and his daughter took up temporary refuge at the tavern of a friend in West Cambridge (known as Menotomy at the time), just outside of Boston. The friend, Mr. Cutter, provided the weather-drenched and weary pair with food and drink, then insisted that they stay for the night until the storm abated.

But Rugg, obdurate, not one to ever heed advice (however reasonable), and vehement when affronted with entreaties, proclaimed prophetically, "Let the storm increase! I will see home to-night in spite of the last tempest—or may I never see home!"

And with that, he was said to hastily usher his daughter into his carriage, give a "whip to his high-spirited horse," then ride off into the tempestuous darkness—with his and

Jenny's human forms never again to be encountered. (Some versions of the story have Rugg getting into a brief physical altercation with his friend before dashing back off into the night.)

He and his daughter never returned home that night— or any night thereafter. Although his tormented wife, his friends, and the authorities searched for days, cycling into fruitless weeks morphing into hopeless months, there was not a remnant of his course—not even a hoofprint—beyond Cutter's tavern.

Not an earthly one, at least.

Soon, the stories began, mere whispers to start, then becoming well-shared legends. Witnesses reported his frantic, transient ghost on roadways and byways throughout New England, seemingly doomed to follow an endless, circuitous path.

On nights that raged with storms, particularly, his wife and neighbors claimed to awaken to the snap of a whip, the familiar echoing thwack of hooves on cobblestones, and the jouncing of a carriage (within the cramped eighteenth-century borders of Boston, homes were built within mere feet of roadways, and with insulation a not-yet-invented luxury, passing vehicles would shake houses "like an earthquake," as Austin noted). Middle Street residents were said to spy with their lanterns Rugg's phosphorescent form, vainly attempting to halt his chaise at last at his front door.

In the decades following his disappearance, his specter has been seen riding aimlessly throughout New England in search of the path home—appearing abruptly, always racing, never stopping, each time bringing forth a brief but intense storm that is said to relentlessly pursue him. Stagecoach drivers, men on horseback, pedestrians, and peddlers alike have claimed to have seen him passing toward or away from Boston, as well as on roadways in Newburyport, Connecticut ("passing through the country like a streak of chalk," as Austin wrote), New Hampshire, Rhode Island, and even on a racetrack in Virginia.

Sometimes he has reportedly stopped briefly to explain his predicament and entreat, "Pray direct me the nearest way to Boston"—then grown irate and dashed off when told the distance. In one well-related instance, after he and his horse repeatedly blew through a toll night after night on the Charlestown Bridge, a frustrated toll taker threw his stool at him.

He has appeared dejected and anxious, he and his daughter made gaunt and weary by time, carriage deteriorated, horse aged and pudgy, its once glossy coat bedraggled and striped with gray. Other times, the steed has said to breathe fire and smell of brimstone, hastily overtaking other carriages.

In some cases he has ultimately found the path back—but still to no avail. After the death of his dejected wife, who never knew the fate that ultimately befell her husband and child, an old woman named Betsey Croft moved into Rugg's house. One night at twilight, she opened the door to a stranger, a child by his side, a "weather-beaten" carriage at the curb. When told that his wife had passed away twenty years earlier, the puzzled Rugg replied, according to Austin, "Though the painting is rather faded, this looks like my house," but noted that it seemed to be on the wrong side of the street. "Indeed, everything here seems to be misplaced," he continued. "The streets are all changed, the people are all changed, the town seems changed."

Years later, when his home, long transformed by the additions, subtractions, loving care, and neglect of ensuing owners, was being auctioned by the state, he was said to appear again. A large throng gathering round him, he asked after his wife, then demanded who had demolished his home, as he did not recognize it in its aged and altered state.

A voice from the crowd, as related by Austin, delivered the bitter news. "Time, which destroys and renews all things, has dilapidated your house. . . . You were cut off from the last age, and you never can be fitted to the present. Your home is gone, and you can never have another home in this world."

So, it is said, Peter Rugg rides still, forever in search of a home and a time long departed, serving as a cautionary tale of how hot heads and haste can leave one lost, following a mislaid path into darkness.

Chapter 27

An Otherworldly Assault

All of a sudden, it began.

An onslaught from beings who appeared and disappeared at a whim, adversaries who could be temporarily shot down but not ultimately felled. Jeering, chasing, cornering, relentlessly besieging, attacking with weapons and projectiles.

So went the months-long, unexplained, spectral assault on the residents of Gloucester in the summer of 1692.

Because it was the year that launched Salem's notorious witch hunt, and with an epidemic of attacks by Native Americans and French raiders amid King William's War (the North American theater of the Nine Years War between France and much of Europe and England that ended in 1697), townspeople assumed—naturally—that they were facing terrestrial assailants.

But they soon came to believe that they were dealing with something much more malevolent and unworldly—devilish, vile, phantasmal.

The first stirrings were in mid-July; inside his home with his family one night, twenty-five-year-old fisherman and farmer Ebenezer Babson suddenly heard bizarre noises, approaching and receding footsteps, taunting cries. They were impossible to catch up with or capture, and they carried what he described as glowing guns.

When the barrage didn't cease—and Babson, upon returning to his home after an errand, heard his pursuers fleeing and proclaiming that they planned to take his house—he fled with his petrified family to the town garrison.

Other beleaguered families soon joined him. While sheltered there, they were plagued by mysterious ethereal noises, voices chanting and chattering in exotic tongues, phantom footsteps (sometimes marching), lurking shadows, and, finally, a horizontal rain of items hurled by invisible hands.

As a suspicious portent, the freakish intrusion occurred along with what strikingly appeared to be an Indian bow and a severed scalp on the bright, alabaster face of the moon.

Turning to the offensive, the town sought reinforcements and began to battle their mystifying enemy—just how many of whom was unclear.

Outside the garrison house, the men of the town attacked six of the strangers. Babson himself triumphantly shot down three of them, but was shocked and horrified when, inexplicably, they soon thereafter rose as if completely unhurt and fled. Sometimes, after being fired upon, they would get back to their feet and simply disappear.

In other cases, they taunted Babson by laying a charm on his gun so it would not properly fire; there were also an immoderate amount of misfires when residents had the creatures within their sights. The odd beings seemed rather hapless themselves; they would repeatedly fire at a target and miss, and they were also spotted queerly circling an empty house, repetitively hitting it with a stick.

Soon, the Gloucester men came to the realization that these invaders were nonphysical specters, inhuman, fiends looking to spread moral perversion, ambushers of Satan who left no footprints (even in the muddiest of soil), incapable of hurting or being hurt. As superstitious Puritans, the townspeople saw the world as full of auguries and warnings, a testing ground of their faith and purity.

Soon a reverend from Gloucester wrote a pleading letter to Puritan forefather Cotton Mather in Boston; he described "rollicking apparitions" and "diabolical revelry." He ultimately concluded that the devil and "his agents" were to blame for all the "molestations" befalling the town, and entreated Mather to pray "that those apparitions may not prove the sad omens of some future and more horrible molestations."

Testing the belief that the unwanted visitors were unGodly demons, a captain keeping guard with several soldiers over their barracks watched as they approached; he nimbly tore a silver button from his coat, rammed it into the barrel of his gun, and fired.

And the beings vanished.

But, vexingly, they returned once again a short while later; this time, upon seeing them, several soldiers dropped to their knees, clasped their hands, closed their eyes, and prayed.

The odd entities disappeared once again.

This time for good.

Over the years, there have been many theories as to what, exactly, caused this lingering, agitating "league of specters"—were they truly agents of the devil? A collective delusion caused by the frenzied, monopolizing witch trials just outside their borders? Or something else defying explanation?

Much as it was for the Gloucesterians 320-plus years ago in the young, uncultivated "New" World, the answer will likely forever remain elusive—taking its place beside thousands of other untold, anonymous mysteries.

Chapter 28

Revenge Is Best Served ... with Blunt Force?

The beaten and dismembered bits of the body were discovered stashed throughout the laboratory. The torso was stuffed into a tea chest smudged a sickly red color by its grisly contents; the jawbone (false teeth and all) was unearthed among ash and other bones burned clear of flesh in the furnace; an assortment of other sections of the chopped and severed body were stuffed cruelly into the toilet (then known by the more dainty title of "privy").

Such was the fate of Dr. George Parkman, a retired, beloved benefactor and Boston Brahmin, as members of the city's traditional upper class were known. When the member of one of Boston's most prosperous families suddenly went missing in November 1849, the alarmed city was said to put out tens of thousands of missing person fliers, and friends and associates searched unflaggingly. Then, within a week of his murder, his butchered remains were found by an enterprising janitor.

The city was horrified. What had happened? How had such a respected member of the community been dealt such a hideous fate?

It wasn't long before the culprit was identified—a revelation almost as surprising as the discovery of Parkman's maimed body. The suspect was John White Webster, a seemingly mild-mannered, decorated, and revered professor of chemistry and geology at Harvard Medical College.

The trial—and Webster's consummate hanging—became one of the most sensational in Boston history, emphasizing the point that even aristocrats aren't immune from horrific, dastardly deeds.

Ultimately, as is the case with many things in life, it all came down to money.

Parkman was a well-known lender and landlord, as well as a donor to Harvard medical school and other prominent institutions and causes. At some point, he provided a substantial loan to Webster in the amount of $2,432, according to PBS's *American Experience*. Over the years, he was able to repay some of his debt, but not all. In November 1849, Parkman, patience tried, came calling for it while on a regular round of debt collecting. He was last seen entering Webster's laboratory at Harvard Medical College on the afternoon of November 23, 1849.

There, according to Webster's confession, the money lender began "gesticulating in the most violent and menacing manner." In a desperate frenzy of rage that he later claimed was self-defense, Webster attacked Parkman, grabbing the nearest blunt instrument—a walking stick—and clubbing him to death. As he confirmed, according to an article from *American Experience*, "there was nothing to break the force of the blow. He fell instantly upon the pavement. There was no second blow. He did not move."

At once repulsed and panicked by what he'd done, he then chopped up Parkman's body, doing a messy job of it and frantically stashing limbs and sections wherever he could.

That same afternoon, Ephraim Littlefield, a janitor in the building (and also an alleged body snatcher) attempted to enter Webster's study but found it locked from the inside. He also heard the sound of incessant running water.

Instantly suspicious once it was announced that Parkman had disappeared, Littlefield began spying on Webster and stealthily chipped away at the wall under the professor's private toilet on the afternoon of Thanksgiving. The next day, he broke through to find bones in the room, which he immediately reported.

Despite the staunch support of his friends and colleagues, Webster was arrested, tried, and found guilty. On August 30, 1850, he was hanged in the city's Leverett Square (once the site of a prison) for his dreadful actions.

And more than 165 years later, so it's said, Parkman still makes his rounds. Particularly, he is believed to haunt his former home on 33 Beacon Street, a four-story Greek Revival brick mansion that was bequeathed to the city by his son, George F. Parkman. Dying a recluse, seemingly forever disturbed by his father's death, he was said to stare out at squirrels frolicking on the Boston Common for hours. He had so much affection for the bold and mischievous creatures that he commissioned a chandelier of bronze squirrels that remains hanging to this day in the second-floor parlor.

On the eerily coincidental date of November 23, 1999— exactly 150 years after his murder—and in an equally fitting disaster involving a toilet, Parkman was said to make his presence known. After a tank burst in the historic house, according to paranormal author Sam Baltrusis, a third-floor toilet overflowed with streams of water, damaging three floors. The incident prompted former employee Cecily Foster, who oversaw the mansion's renovation in the 1990s, to remark to the *Boston Globe*, "Maybe the ghost of Dr. Parkman came to visit last night."

Some believe that he most definitely did.

Ultimately, the lurid case serves as a rather horrendous reminder of the importance of paying our debts.

Chapter 29

Lizzie Borden
Took an . . .

You know the rest don't you? If not, you're probably not the kind to be drawn to this type of book—but just in case the age-old nursery rhyme somehow slipped by you, pay a visit to dear-old Lizzie. She'd be more than happy to tell you, maybe even give you a demonstration.

She was a spinster—age thirty-two, a veritable old maid at the time—who was accused of the particularly savage murders in 1892 of her father, Andrew, and stepmother, Abby, in the (then) prosperous mill town of Fall River. Although publicly condemned, she was eventually acquitted in a case that became infamous around the world, inspiring the catchy ditty that had her dealing her father forty whacks and her stepmother forty-one. (In actuality, Andrew Borden sustained ten or eleven blows, while Abby Borden endured twenty, as estimated by forensic examinations at the time.)

The Fall River home that was the location of the murders, fifty miles south of Boston close to the Rhode Island border, is now a bed-and-breakfast. Attracting murder aficionados as well as many a steady flux of paranormal investigators—or just many of those, who, 120 years later, are simply intrigued by the gruesome, unsolved slayings and the trial surrounding them that gripped the attention of the world—its current owners readily tout its grisly history and its abundant spectral activity.

The inn sleeps up to eighteen; guests can stay in Lizzie or Emma (her sister) "suites," Andrew and Abby's master bedroom (where it's said that the ghost of the miserly businessman can be placated with money left on a bureau), the quarters of maid Bridget Sullivan, the guest room where Abby's slaughtered body was discovered, Abby's dressing room, as was well as rooms named for Lizzie's lawyer, Andrew Jennings, and district attorney Hosea Knowlton.

"Ghost cams" that require a subscription run on a regular rotation (when the rooms are unoccupied), séances are regularly held on-site, and those guests brave enough to stay overnight have reported varied supernatural encounters, ranging from objects moving and doors opening and closing when no hands have been near and no drafts were evident, to mysterious sounds, shadows, overpowering scents of flowers, whispers, weeping, and footsteps in areas where no human forms are known to be. Some have even claimed to have been touched and caressed—or felt an ear tugged by wicked hands—awoken at night to a distinct presence sitting on the bed (a marked depression left behind when lights are flicked back on), or experience an overwhelming, frigid mass of air.

Some guests, according to co-owner and manager Lee-ann Wilber, have been so spooked that they'll simply take off in the middle of the night like the family from *The Amityville Horror* (but, she stressed, no refunds are given for fraidy-cats).

"It's a very active house," she said in an interview.

Making it a natural (or, rather, unnatural?) draw for paranormal researchers.

Dozens of teams—including the crews from Syfy's *Ghost Hunters* and the Travel Channel's *Ghost Adventures*—have claimed to have captured orbs, light streaks, electronic voice phenomena (EVP), and contact through what are known as "spirit boxes," and in other instances they have had their equipment and cameras inconceivably tampered with. In more poltergeisty experiences, tables have purportedly hovered and rotated during séances, and some visiting mediums have even been said to channel Abby at the time of her death, falling to the floor to writhe and flail.

Meanwhile, many a photo has been taken by lovers of the macabre, slumped like Andrew Borden on a love seat in the parlor, or lying supplant on the floor like Abby. Those who want to take it even further can exchange vows on the murder grounds.

That's right—you can get married there.

Couples will sometimes dress up in gothic or turn-of-the-century costumes, according to Wilber; or they'll come in the accustomed white dress and tux. Very often, though, a hatchet will be used to cut the cake.

"It's a typical wedding," Wilber jested in an interview. "It just takes place in a room where a man got murdered."

That killing occurred on the morning of August 4, 1892, with both victims ambushed with axes. Abby, in the upstairs guest room, was the first to get literally whacked; according to forensic evidence, she was struck with a hatchet while facing her attacker, who then chopped and slashed the back of her head until it was nearly severed. A short while later, the culprit (or culprits) then murdered Andrew by striking him directly in the face with a hatchet as he was in the sitting room. It's suggested that he was napping when the fatal blows were delivered. Adding to the repulsive nature of the killings, the two bodies were given autopsies in probably the most unappetizing of places—in the middle of the dining room.

Perhaps one of the reasons the case became such a cause célèbre, as some have termed it—and remains that way to this day—is due to the overzealousness of the murders. Andrew Borden's head was literally made concave and unrecognizable due to the hatchet attack to his face—those with a curiosity in the macabre can readily find images of their maimed bodies: Andrew's long, lean body clad in black and slumped on a love seat, Abby's corpulent form face down on the floor.

Lizzie was arrested just a week later, her trial taking place the following summer, ending rather quickly in a shocking acquittal. She never took the stand in her own defense yet faithfully claimed her innocence, and it's still not known today with 100 percent certainty whether she was in fact the culprit. The conspiracy theories are almost as plenteous as those surrounding the assassination of President John F. Kennedy, pointing fingers at, among others, her older sister, Emma, who was out of town at the time; a longtime maid; robbers; jilted business associates (Andrew Borden was known for frugality that bordered on stinginess); illegitimate sons; and an uncle who stayed in the house the night before the killings.

Nevertheless, the spinster was shunned by the community much like Nathaniel Hawthorne's Hester Prynne; she relocated to another Fall River home that she named "Maplecroft" and remained unmarried—particularly due to her friendship with noted silent movie actress Nance O'Neil, rumors were rife that she was a lesbian. She died of pneumonia in 1927 at age sixty-six and today rests in Fall River's Oak Grove Cemetery in a family plot marked by a large obelisk—not far from her slain father and stepmother; mother, Sarah; and sister, Emma—under a small, curved, inauspicious grave marked simply, "Lizbeth." According to newspaper reports, the monument has been vandalized numerous times, standing as a testament to Lizzie's enduring notoriety.

As for the accused murderess? Besides the occasional disturbance from defilers, she seems sound in her bed several feet below, safeguarding her truths—and, unlike her father, protected in her eternal sleep from unexpected, barbarous hatchet blows.

Chapter 30

Wizards, Fortune Tellers, and Damsels in (Perpetual) Distress

Agonized screeches and peals are said to echo throughout a small cove in Marblehead Harbor. Heard at sporadic intervals, keeping superstitious locals away from the ocean-carved cavern on nights cloaked with dark and fog, they serve as a perpetual reminder of the demise of an Englishwoman at the brutal hands of pirates—and those who were too afraid of losing their own lives to come to her aid.

Marblehead was once described as "the greatest town for fishing in New England," according to Pam Matthias Peterson, executive director of the Marblehead Museum and Historical Society; as a fantastical legend goes, the harbor was so populous with such immense fish that a person could walk from one side of to the other on the fishes' backs without suffering even a splash of water to the shoe.

Sometime in the 1800s or 1900s, pirates trolling the local waters of the Atlantic captured a Spanish ship after the town's fishing fleet had departed for the day. Directing it into the quietude and privacy of the small Lovis Cove, they then set about their compassionless plunder, killing everyone on board, including, it was said, a beautiful Englishwoman. Although she tried to fight them off, according to Peterson, they murdered her in the cove, chopping her fingers clean from her hands to get at her fine rings. As she was being defiled, she screamed over and over until she was ultimately quieted forever: "Mercy! Lord save me!" The locals, terrified of the pirates who freely roamed the shores, heard her but were unable—or unwilling—to help. It's said that she continues her ghostly wails to this day, perhaps forever bemoaning the languor of locals who merely listened to her in her death throes.

Much like its neighbor Salem, the affluent seaside town of Marblehead—shaped like a mitt gripping the Atlantic, its stately homes clustered like keepers along its mosaic of ever-so-narrow streets—also has its legends of mysticism. It was, in fact, part of Salem until 1649, and at least one of its less desirable residents, Wilmot Redd, was carted off to the adjacent town during its infamously consuming witch hysteria of 1692. There, like nearly two dozen others, she suffered the deathly grip of the noose.

Most notably: Retired ship's captain Edward Dimond—or "Old Dimond," as he was fittingly known due to his antiquity—and his world-renowned, clairvoyant granddaughter Moll were revered for their knowledge of things to which most of us stand oblivious.

Old Dimond fashioned himself a wizard, and convinced many others of this as well, so much so that they sought his help and that of his assumed magical powers in resolving disputes such as theft or mistreatment of the defenseless. It was also said that he had the ability to tame the sea and the elements to bring local sailors and vessels safely back to shore; during storms, he would be seen pacing the town's Old Burial Hill, which offers a vantage of the harbor, scolding and daring the winds much like King Lear famously did of his tempest.

Eclipsing his notoriety, however, was his granddaughter Moll's talents. Immortalized after her death in an early poem by John Greenleaf Whittier, simply titled "Moll Pitcher," she relocated to Lynn upon marriage and became quickly revered for her stunningly accurate ability to read the future. The prospectors, the lovelorn, the ill-fortuned, the needy, the famous, the curious, and those embarking on impending voyages came from all over to hear their possible futures. It was said that "royalty of Europe, as well as simple maids of America, sought to learn the future from her," according to Peterson. She was rumored to have foretold the Battle of Bunker hill, and, upon a visit to George Washington in Cambridge, she spoke of his eventual victory in the Revolutionary War, as reported by Peterson. Remarkably, after losing her husband, she was so renowned that she was able to support her four children with her talents, which she did with cards and reading palms and tea leaves.

What set both her and her grandfather apart from others with purportedly divine powers was the fact that they were champions of the poor—call them soothsaying Robin Hoods of sorts.

Chapter 31
Driven to Disaster

Just due to its very nature as a small, densely populated, historic state that prospered out of agriculture, Massachusetts is traced with a number of roads that are eerie in the daytime, let alone when merely lit by the arc of headlights on a dark night. Streets slicing through its more rural areas take the place of former meandering centuries-old buggy routes and cow paths—very often unspotted by street lights, beset with sharp curves, trees, and woods whose forward motion has been shunted by the steady progress of two-lane blacktop slowly edging in. But some roads, just like houses, boats, hospitals, schools, or even entire towns, are much more ominous than others. (And ever drive in Boston during rush hour? That's enough to terrify anyone.)

Such is the case with Dudley Road in Billerica, a medium-sized town just northwest of Boston and adjacent to Lowell, the self-described "Birthplace of the American Industrial Revolution." Starting out as two lanes that winnow down to a narrow path that is a horror itself to car shocks and struts, many ghostly apparitions have been seen walking its length; most notably, nuns. As the story goes, much like the plot of a sadistic Lucio Fulci movie—the 1980 *City of the Living Dead*, in which a priest kills himself to open the gates of hell, comes to mind—there once was a nunnery on the road. (The Saint Thecla Retreat House, private property of the one-hundred-year-old international community Daughters of St. Paul, is still located there.)

Three of its resident nuns who had taken vows espousing themselves to Jesus Christ were, instead of pursuing spiritual awakening, discovered to be working as agents of the devil by practicing witchcraft. It was said that they fled down the road but were soon apprehended and hanged. (The local Daughters of St. Paul community denies the story.)

Supposedly, a house that was either where the trio practiced their dark arts or was later built upon the location where they were strung up and hanged without a trial—the stories vary—was abandoned years ago because it began being literally consumed by the earth, sinking deeper and deeper into the ground up to its second-story windows. Photos of the purported property snapped by paranormal-seeking explorers show a once-white building, paint grayed and pared away by the elements, with a brick chimney and a steeply pitched roof. It's difficult to tell whether it is, in fact, sinking, or merely overwhelmed by its verdant environs.

According to Ron Kolek of the New England Ghost Project, another nun was said to be struck by a car and hurled into a tree while walking the road; legend says that if you take a picture of that tree, you might capture her anguished face within its bark.

Visitors have claimed to see strange hovering lights and ghostly nuns walking along the road—which was more of a draw before additional houses were erected along its length—and hear, in the nearby woods, crying, moaning, and the shaking of chains.

Other rumors—that many fluff off as merely that—tell of an insane asylum and the butchering and debauchery of nuns by an escaped inmate.

Nearby, Beaver Brook Road in the small town of Littleton is said to be roamed by the wraith of a farmer. The stories were so numerous that a local newspaper researched the claim, finding that a farmer had once been killed on the road.

Meanwhile, south of town, inside an axis of prominent paranormal activity known as the "Bridgewater Triangle," two phantoms are said to terrorize cars that dare whir down them. First, there's the "Red-Headed Hitchhiker of Route 44," said to be a burly man in jeans and a plaid shirt with an ample beard and a shaggy thicket of bright red hair. According to filmmakers Aaron Cadieux and Manny Famolare, as the urban legend goes, the drifter will show up seated in cars if there's an extra empty seat, or if drivers turn their lights off, honk three times, then flick their lights back on; he's also said to manipulate the radio to music of his liking.

Meanwhile, the "Mad Trucker of Copicut Road" is decidedly more aggressive. The seven-mile, mostly unpaved road slices through Freetown and its state forest, and it's said that drivers traveling down it have been overtaken by a pickup truck that seemingly appears from nowhere, beeping, flashing its lights, running them into ditches—then disappearing just as suddenly.

But the story raises skepticism in even the most devout of believers. "I've never found someone who had firsthand knowledge," noted paranormal expert Jeff Belanger told Cadieux and Famolare in their 2013 documentary, *The Bridgewater Triangle*. "It's just a story that people pass around."

But, he added, "The story's so good, we keep talking about it."

The only way to find out if the stories are, in fact, true? Take a drive down any of these roads—that is, if you dare.

Part 8

WHERE EVIL PERVADES

"Can an entire city be haunted?"

So posits a character in Stephen King's 1986 tome **It** *(a treatise on the everlasting bonds of childhood, as well as an indubitable nightmare for coulrophobics, or those with a paralyzing fear of clowns).*

Some would most definitely answer yes—and profess that not just cities, but entire geographic areas, can be plagued by nefarious and calamitous presences as permeating and aged as time itself.

Chapter 32
The Bewitched City

"Damn you—I curse you and Salem!"

With the last ragged, suffocated remnant of breath left in his crushed body, Giles Corey laboriously spat out these fateful final words.

The cantankerous, mulish octogenarian, accused of being a wizard, was pressed to death in what was one of the most notoriously heinous executions of the Salem witch trials of 1692.

And it was said that his spiteful malediction has plagued the city ever since.

Still, some contend that the evil in this small coastal community permeates much deeper than the last-gasping omen of an old man.

It was Witch City–based author and educator Margaret Press who first came up with the term the "Salem factor," referring to the overabundance of abnormalities and eerie phenomena pervading the city's limits.

Some have surmised that a potential electrical fault running beneath the Salem area gives rise to its panoply of bizarre and unexplained happenings. The natives, for their part, believed it was something much more sinister. The Naumkeag Native Americans who lived throughout the Northeast—and whose name, discordantly with Salem at least, means "peace"—were purportedly convinced that the land around the fated city was infused with a negative energy and talked of a presence both visual and tangible.

As Press attests, "The devil once lived here."
Or perhaps still does.

THE INFAMOUS TRIALS

You simply can't talk about Salem without discussing its scandalous witch hunt, one of the most prominent cases of ruthless inquisition, scapegoating, fearmongering, and mass hysteria in the country's past.

It was that very episode that in many ways has served to define Salem—much as the city initially attempted to wipe away the dark stain of its history (but which it now embraces for its historical and otherworldly qualities, most particularly through its thriving mystic and paranormal commerce, as well as its month-long Halloween celebration, Haunted Happenings). An unsettling condemnation of human nature and a testament to the overwhelming powers of group persuasion, the remnants of the historical event—both real and spectral—continue to linger across the centuries.

It all began, as the story goes, with late nights of debauchery. Local girls were said to gather in secret with a Caribbean slave named Tituba in the kitchen of what was assumed to be an otherwise sanctimonious home—that of the respected Rev. Samuel Parris. Supposedly flirting with dark arts such as voodoo that the slave imported from her native isles, the virtuous, pious Puritan maidens were soon witnessed dancing in the dark woods, and were reported to scream uncontrollably, collapse into fits, yap like dogs, complain of painful piercing and pricking sensations without origin, and crumple into unresponsive, comatose states.

The terrified townspeople, unquestioning in their belief of both good and evil vying for control of the human realm, and living an unsettled life in the wild unrest of the late seventeenth century (their daily fears including the threat of attacking Native Americans, decimating infectious diseases, and outbursts of war from competing factions of Europe as they shifted borders and signed a roulette of treaties), believed the young women were possessed or hexed.

Immediately, they suspected witchcraft. Local doctors, reverends, and lawmen were soon entreated for assistance from frantic mothers, fathers, friends, and other relatives. Time only served to accelerate the collective symptoms of a growing number of girls in the village that at that time populated several hundred; more and more began to fall ill and exhibit signs of being entangled in the devil's clutches—or that of his dark servants.

Soon, accusations were slung and arrests made. Tituba was among one of the first to be implicated. Most likely as a means of self-preservation, the slave woman admitted to being guilty, confessing to signing her name in the devil's book, flying through the air on sticks, and naming, in the process, four prominent town women who were also in league with the devil.

With that, the hunt officially began.

Playing to a larger and larger audience, the afflicted girls grew in number and accelerated their hysterics, soon before the court. More and more people were brought up for scrutiny, with gossip, hearsay, and outright assumptions readily accepted as evidence (much of it no doubt prompted by long-standing grudges and general ill will, property or livestock disputes, or religious differences).

Some of the accused confessed; others were jailed for adamantly professing their innocence; all were examined for strange marks, "puckers and blemishes and the telltale false teats that mark a witch," as John Updike described in his contemporary tale of bedevilment in New England, *The Witches of Eastwick*. With time, accusations intensified and consumed more and more in a ripple effect.

Ultimately, in a span of just six frenzied months, nineteen men and women were hanged (as well as two dogs believed to be accomplices to their conjuring masters), Corey was hideously pressed, and dozens of others suffered in fetid confines in the Witches Gaol (a British term for "jail") on Federal Street. The dungeon was not equipped with bars, but a deterrent for attempted escape was a consummate hanging death, according to Sam Baltrusis, author of *Ghosts of Salem: Haunts of the Witch City*. Despite their debasement and inability to perform their livelihoods or see their families or friends, prisoners were billed to help pay for the salaries of the sheriff, magistrate, and hangman, as well as the cuffs and shackles that constantly bound them. They were furthermore charged for "luxuries" such as straw, bedding, and food (if they could afford them) and were habitually denied water as a means to extract confessions. Those that did make it out alive were often left destitute, their properties taken over by the county or the state.

The several that didn't, meanwhile, were taken by oxcart to Gallows Hill and hung by the neck before crowds of spectators. The site of the killing ground had been obscured by the ages (some say purposely by ashamed locals hoping time would blanch the embarrassing bloodletting from historical record). But just recently, proving the enduring fascination with the historic hysterics, a group of scholars identified an overgrown area known as Proctor's Ledge as the exact location of the hangings. The discovery came about through a years-long project that included studying maps, court records, and aerial photographs, as well as the use of ground-penetrating radar. Previously a few theories as to its location included a public copse between the current Proctor and Pope Streets, according to Baltrusis, a wooded hill littered with trash behind a Walgreen's on Boston Street, a site adjacent to the North River, or—in a striking contrast—a town playground jarringly called Gallows Hill Park just near downtown where skeletal fragments have supposedly been discovered.

It was believed that the bodies of the executed were unceremoniously dumped in a shallow ditch. Only a few were given proper burials, including that of elderly farmer George Jacobs, tavern keeper and farmer John Proctor (protagonist of Arthur Miller's classic 1953 play *The Crucible*), and Rebecca Nurse, whose son was said to recover her body by the shawl of night, rowing her downriver to her homestead.

The final executions took place in late September 1692, and by March of the following year, the voracious blood lust appeared to ebb away as once-subtle gnaws of doubt bit harder at the public conscious. Due also to waning interest, as well as the rumor that key witnesses simply absconded in the night, the trials finally ended, and all prisoners were released and absolved.

Before long, the people of Salem grew ashamed and rancorous of the entire affair, having lost so many of their own under tenuous circumstances in the frenetic whirlwind that consumed the town.

Still, its victims weren't so quick to dismiss it—or to allow themselves to be forgotten.

COREY'S CURSE

One of Salem's most prominent residents—and whose last words would be immortalized in American history—

eighty-year-old Goodman "Giles" Corey was a prosperous, thrice-married farmer known for his blunt and truculent nature. As the tempest of the trials grew ever stormier, the time for his scrutiny inevitably came.

Deemed a "dreadful wizard" with an assaulting and abusive specter, he was hauled away and locked up. But, being shrewd and laconic, he only declared that he was "not guilty," refusing to stand trial or make any other comment. It was later speculated that his silence arose out of his recognition of the futility of resistance and the knowledge that if he escaped conviction, his estate could be bequest to his heirs as his will intended, rather than confiscated by the state.

But remaining mute only sparked the ire of his tormentors; they deemed that he would be put to a *peine forte et dure*, French for "hard and forceful punishment."

On September 19, 1692, after months languishing in the putrid town dungeon, he was stripped down, and his chained, naked, haggard, filthy body was dragged to a freshly dug pit not far from the jail.

There, his captors laid him flat on his back on a wooden plank.

"Will you submit to be tried?"

The inquiry came from Jonathan Corwin, high sheriff of Essex County, who was crouched above him.

The stoic Corey gave no answer.

In a high-stakes match of grit and stamina, Corwin raised Corey's silence by having his men sandwich the old man's body with a top plank—then laying upon it a growing pile of various-sized rocks, stones, and boulders. The excruciating proceeding continued for two days. More and more slabs and rubble were added; the diminishing old man was allowed only mouthfuls of bread and trickling sips of water; the unyielding and unforgiving magistrate interjecting at intervals, "Do you submit?"

But irresolute, Corey still gave no reply. All that could be heard were his wheezing, superficial breaths; the scraping and shifting of rock upon rock as he took the shallowest gulps that the weight deforming and splintering his bones, caving in his chest and stomach, would allow.

Finally, in what Corwin believed was ultimate triumph, Corey's lips formed a soundless whisper. Leaning close, the sheriff waited for the lamenting plea from his elderly prisoner. But the old man stubbornly forsook his executioner, famously declaring, "More weight!"

His request thus immediately granted, the eighty-year-old's face was said to flush crimson, his eyes bulged, tongue protruded, and, with the last iota of vigor in his pulverized body, he lent his infamous curse to the sheriff and to Salem.

And, it seems, he was avenged—many times over.

Just four years later, in 1696, the ruthless Corwin died prematurely of a heart attack. By then, with the community loath to even speak about the trials, the lawman who once held such sway over the circus-like proceedings was reviled. Afraid that his body would be desecrated, his family buried Corwin temporarily in the basement of his home—now the Joshua Ward House on Washington Street—before eventually quietly relocating it to the Broad Street Cemetery.

Ensuing sheriffs and keepers of the Salem jail met similar early demises; nearly all of them were said to die as the result of heart problems or ailments of the blood.

Still, that succession of bad tidings doesn't seem to have fully appeased Corey's spirit. It is said that his apparition, which has been seen floating among the tombstones of the

Howard Street Burying Ground adjacent to the old jail, is a portent of bad tidings.

One of Salem's most significant twentieth-century disasters was the great fire of 1914; consuming 1,376 buildings over 250 acres, it displaced tens of thousands who sought temporary, chaotic refuge on the Salem common, and resulted in the loss of lives and millions of dollars in damage and commerce. Although it began with explosions at the Korn Leather Factory (a building without sprinklers), the superstitious called it the telltale work of Corey, whose maimed, disfigured spirit was witnessed patrolling the Howard Street cemetery that day. His vindictive presence has been said to presage other natural and unnatural disasters over the years, as well. Howard Street is where Corey's specter can most commonly be seen and felt; visitors to the old burial ground have reported heart palpitations or a heavy, stifling sensation in their chest—Corey perhaps, all these centuries later, still stubborn in his silence, not yet avenged for his horrendous death.

THE DAMNED UNITED

But Corey's wasn't the only curse bespoken in Salem.

Sarah Good was another condemned "witch" hanged in July 1692. A salty, pipe-smoking beggar who engaged in minor acts of mischief when she felt slighted (such as petty thievery or releasing penned animals), she was soon among the accused. Although pregnant, she was jailed—her baby coming into the world and dying within the walls of the grimy prison—and her own preteen daughter was bullied into testifying against her.

As she was headed to the gallows, Salem's second minister, Nicholas Noyes, attempted to coax a confession.

Much like Corey, she was steadfast in her innocence, but with a much more caustic tongue. Calling him a liar, she proclaimed, "I am no more a witch than you are a wizard. And if you take away my life, God will give you blood to drink."

Several years later, Noyes suffered an internal hemorrhage. Bleeding profusely from his mouth, he literally choked on his own blood.

A LINGERING MALICE

One of the city's first brick houses, the Joshua Ward House on Washington Street was built on the site of the former home of Judge Jonathan Corwin. Callous and known for his cruel methods—his nickname was "the Strangler" because of his penchant for extracting confessions by that means, Corwin was known for tying accused witches into contorted positions in which their neck and heels unnaturally touched—it is said that he continues to carry out his malicious deeds to this day. According to author Holly Mascott Nadler, visitors to the historic property have reported a sensation of being touched, pushed, brushed, or throttled about the neck by unseen hands.

Corwin's adversary Corey is also believed to make mischief as a means of eternally harassing his murderer. His enduring presence has been said to throw various items, set off alarms, melt candles (although they were never lit), unfurl documents before disbelieving eyes, and manifest himself in persistent cold spots.

But the elegant Federal-style mansion may have more than those eternally embittered, battling ghosts haunting its halls. Built in 1784, the house is also where an unsuspecting real estate agent snapped a Polaroid of an eerie specter, what some believers consider one of the creepiest, and best local examples of, a photo capturing a spirit. Dark and slightly blurred, it shows what appears to be the ghost of a woman standing in front of a door; wearing a long black dress, ivory white hands at her sides, her dark hair is a wild, tousled, Medusa-like mass swirling wildly about her solemn face.

A GRAVE BEFITTING A WITCH JUDGE?

Located within the gate of stone and wrought iron, beyond the tumult of the city with its cars and buses, bicyclists and pedestrians, the two skulls glower. Lightly caressed by encroaching climbing vines, an hourglass with ragged wings set between them, they ominously protrude in bas relief from a large rectangular tabletop tomb. About the size of a steamer chest, either side decorated like fluted pillars, the craniums that bedeck it are realistically cadaverous—turned slightly toward one another, nasal cavities and eye sockets dark and hollowed, bone curvature clearly defined.

Coupled with the rambling ivy and the sparse epitaph, the tomb looks like a freaky set decoration from an old black-and-white Universal Monsters film in which Boris Karloff plays a voracious baddie.

In actuality, the elaborate gravestone is the resting place of a real-life villain of sorts: William Stoughton, another of the trials' pitiless arbiters.

Chief justice of the trials, Stoughton was most known for his flippant mistreatment of due process (not to be formally established this side of the Atlantic until the enforcement of the Constitution nearly one hundred years later, but a concept that dates back to the thirteenth-century Magna Carta), as well as his blatant allowance of interjections and acceptance of dubious spectral evidence.

Unlike his contemporaries Corwin and Hathorne, however, he was not so maligned following the scandalously flagrant mockery of justice—nor did he ever apologize for his role, as Samuel Sewall did. Before and after the trials, he called Dorchester, its own incorporated town until it was annexed by Boston, his home. Educated at Harvard University, he served as state governor after the trials, and was even consecrated in name in his alma mater's Stoughton Hall, as well as the south-of-Boston town of Stoughton.

A wealthy landowner when he died, he was interred at Dorchester North Burying Ground (which is also abutted by his namesake Stoughton Street, in an area of the neighborhood also named in his honor) upon his death at age seventy in 1701, according to the Stoughton Historical Society. His stone was simple; his epitaph, believed to be written either by him or by Puritan minister Cotton Mather, was ostentatious. Originally inscribed in Latin, it identified him as "acute in judgment," "a lover of equity," and "a defender of the laws" (Corey, if he weren't said to be endlessly prowling outside of his own grave in Salem, would no doubt be gyrating in it at the thought of those very praises), as well as virtuous, eloquent, elegant, wise, and gracious. "All admire him!" it affirmed, according to historical society records, while also bemoaning "Alas! Alas! What Grief!"

And, for more than 125 years, he lay beneath that braggadocio epitaph—until, in 1828, his tomb was replaced by Harvard, for which by then he had become a significant benefactor. No doubt well-intentioned, the spooky, skull-emblazoned stone that was erected proved much more befitting for the judge known for his mercilessness during the egregious trials.

Hearkening the well-quoted line from Shakespeare's *Julius Caesar*, "The evil that men do lives after them; the good is oft interred with their bones"—it is a chilling reminder that reputations become public domain after death, and that our nefarious deeds catch up with us—even if it takes a century or two.

THE OLDEST GHOSTS

Located on Charter Street and dating to 1637, Burying Point is the city's oldest cemetery. It serves as the final remembrance spot for several witch trial victims. But lying discordantly within their midst is also savage judge John Hathorne (who sent many of them to the gallows and who was so disparaged over time that his descendant, Salem native son Nathaniel Hawthorne, purposely added a *w* to his name as a distancing tactic).

According to legend, a casket once broke straight through the wall of an inn that formerly abutted the burial ground. A willowy lady dressed in white has been spied drifting within its depths (some believe it is Corey's second wife, believed to be his one true love), and visitors passing by or walking through have claimed to have felt an overpowering fog of despair.

Chapter 33
Other Trials

Any town rich in history has its haunts. Beyond the notorious witch hunt, many other resident specters vie for attention in Salem. Among other instances, screams have been heard over landlines; unseen forces have brushed, touched, and pushed the living; and ghosts of colonial sentinels have been seen making rounds they may be obliged to for eternity.

INCARCERATED SPIRITS

Opened in 1813 and in operation for more than 175 years, the legendary Old Salem Jail may have initially been afflicted by extemporaneous energy from Corey's accursed spirit.

Located next to his literal haunting ground, Howard Street Cemetery, it was said some of the salvaged rocks used in its initial construction were still soaked with centuries-old blood from the 1692 executions, according to Baltrusis. In an 1880s expansion, Rockport granite was salvaged from St. Peter Street—not far from the site of Corey's grisly death.

The location of more than fifty of its own hangings, as reported by Baltrusis, the prison housed such disreputable inmates as "Boston Strangler" Albert DeSalvo, feared Mafia hit man Joseph "the Animal" Barboza, and former New England mob boss Gennaro Angiulo.

Before closing down in the 1990s, it was perhaps most known for its wretched conditions and tumultuous atmosphere. In the 1980s, chamber pots were still in use, and prisoners, considered the waste of society, literally waded in their own dregs when several of them, in protest, clamorously upended their makeshift receptacles. (A few inmates successfully sued the county for inhumane conditions.) When they were finally cleared out in 1991, the criminals left a passage of wanton destruction; they smashed windows and televisions and kicked in walls, lit trash on fire, and triumphed with written desecrations of "We won!"

From then on—until, as is the case with many former institutional buildings in the Northeast, no matter how seedy their history, it was transformed into luxury apartments—it sat boarded up and vacant, a gathering spot for squatters and souvenir-seeking vandals. But supernatural stories abounded, as reported by Baltrusis; there were rumors of unearthly, metal-like clinking sounds throughout the abandoned structure, as well as a noted, unnatural heaviness to the air. Some visitors and passersby claimed to see ghosts of moaning Civil War–era soldiers; shadowy figures running across the yard to the chain-link fence as if making their eternal escape; apparitions walking in midair on a floor that no longer existed.

Former prisoners themselves also claimed to have nightmarish run-ins, or even share cells with, their long-dead predecessors—giving a whole new meaning to the concept of a life sentence.

HAWTHORNE'S HAUNTS

Named for the city's native son and author, the Hawthorne Hotel seemed ill-fated from the start. Opened in 1925, it was located on property formerly occupied by the Franklin Building—which, during the 1800s, burned down six times, claiming several lives in the process, according to Baltrusis.

Room 325, in particular, is believed to be host to a long-time, unearthly guest. In one well-known story, a business-man, after being awoken in the night by another patron using his bathroom, mentioned to front desk attendants the next morning that he wasn't aware he was paying for a com-munal washroom. A confused but polite clerk followed him to his room, showing him that there was only one way in and out—so there was no way another guest could have slipped in to use his bathroom in the middle of the night.

Other reports have included disembodied voices and invisible groping hands, and some elevator riders have felt a phantom presence taking the lift alongside them. Faucets have been said to turn on and off on their own—as well as toilets flushing of their own volition—while tables and chairs have miraculously moved themselves just moments after being set and organized. Meanwhile, in the Cabin, the longtime, nautical-themed headquarters of the Salem Maritime Society atop the hotel, various stored charts and records have been discovered in disarray—despite the room being locked the majority of the time.

LITERALLY HAUNTED

Salem-born author Nathaniel Hawthorne, celebrated for his unflinching commentary on morality and class distinction in early America, was a regular visitor to the Turner-Ingersoll Mansion. The distinctly characteristic 1668 dark clapboard house, with its three chimneys and numerous gables, served as inspiration for the author's 1851 *The House of the Seven Gables*.

Some say its many rooms and dark passages are haunted by longtime resident Susan Ingersoll, Hawthorne's cousin. Although photography isn't allowed inside the historic colonial building, many visitors, while snapping photos outside, have purportedly captured pictures of her peering out of its many windows. Others have claimed to see her roaming around inside. Now a museum, the building is also said to be haunted by the tempestuous ghost of a little boy who can be heard running around in the attic.

As for Hawthorne? Much as he was in life, his spirit remains calm and contemplative.

Chapter 34
The (Other) Triangle

It was late in the night, quiet and still, the neighborhood absorbed in sleep.

Raynham resident William Russo was walking his dog, Samantha, along a set of power lines near his house. The typical half-mile loop, like always. Nothing unusual.

Then, all of a sudden, Samantha's demeanor abruptly changed. She began to tug, agitated, at her leash, shaking, quivering—as he described it, "rattlin' like an old Chevy."

What had her spooked? He looked and listened, bewildered.

Then he finally heard it. A kind of high-pitched wail, a primitive language foreign to his ears. "Eh wan chu. Eh wan chu. Keahr. Keahr."

And just a moment later, he identified the source.

A few feet away, bathed in a circle of dim streetlight, stood a creature unlike anything he'd ever seen: hairy, unclothed, potbellied, eyes huge, standing upright, just three to four feet tall.

After the fear subsided—and he was back safely in his home—he struggled to make sense of what he'd seen. He considered himself a skeptic, not the type to believe in otherworldly phenomena.

Finally he came to the conclusion that, whatever the bizarre being was, it seemed to be beckoning him, trying to lure him into the light for whatever reason—benevolent or malevolent.

Its repeated screech could be a guttural attempt at an enticement: "We want you, we want you . . . come here, come here."

But he'll never know for sure, because he didn't happen upon the creature—or it on him—again. And he's since moved out of the neighborhood where he had the strange encounter with the curious biped.

These are the sorts of stories—seemingly countless and varied, bizarre, unexplained, and often terrifying—that are rife within the so-called Bridgewater Triangle, a notorious hotbed of phenomena just outside Boston.

A swath of land whose borders shift depending on whom you're talking to, the Triangle is considered one of the most haunted places not only in greater Boston, but in the entire state of Massachusetts. Drawing those fascinated by the unknown, it has been the subject of numerous books and a full-length documentary, and has attracted paranormal researchers from around the world.

The two-hundred-square-mile area, which stretches roughly from Abington to Freetown to Rehoboth, thus embodying a rough triangle shape—again, an area considered by many to be elastic—is profuse with unexplained phenomena. Within its mysterious depths, there have been purported sightings of Bigfoot and UFOs, all manner of eerie apparitions, bloodthirsty wild dogs, inexplicable creatures, and birds and snakes the shapes and sizes of their prehistoric ancestors, among other odd and unusual wonders such as archaeological and geological oddities and primitive etchings. A draw for the darker side of humanity, it has also been the site of satanic rituals, murders, grave robbings—and an unusual number of people have disappeared within its wilds.

"It's becoming one of the preeminent paranormal stories in the world," Tim Weisberg, host of the radio show *Spooky Southcoast*, told filmmakers Manny Famolare and Aaron Cadieux in their award-winning 2013 documentary on the infamous area.

As a nod to the world-renowned Bermuda Triangle—the relentless devourer of so many aircraft and ships—the area was given its name in 1983 by cryptozoologist Loren Coleman. (Cryptozoology is the study of creatures whose existence has not yet been proven due to a lack of evidence—such as Bigfoot or the Loch Ness Monster.)

And the expert on the unknown believes unfailingly in the Triangle's host of wonders. "I don't believe in the Bridgewater Triangle—I accept it," he asserted to Famolare and Cadieux.

The majority of stories, sightings, and odd experiences proliferate from two distinct areas: the Freetown–Fall River State Forest, and the roughly 17,000-acre Hockomock Swamp, which spans Bridgewater, East Bridgewater, Easton, Norton, Raynham, and Taunton.

According to Weisberg, "Hockomock" was Algonquin for "place where spirits dwell," and it became a hiding place for natives after the late seventeenth-century King Philip's War. It is said to be host to thousands of unmarked graves.

Although its origins are hotly debated, many attribute the Triangle's pervasive overabundance of unexplained activity to the mistreatment of the Native American population during that colonial-era war. Erupting in 1675 in Swansea in response to invading Europeans, the local natives under Metacomet (King Philip) rebelled. The battle was brutal and fierce on both sides, with Metacomet initially gaining a short-lived advantage.

By that fall, several colonies were involved, with entire villages destroyed, noncombative men and innocent women and children wantonly slaughtered, and, ultimately, 5 percent of the region's population—both natives and settlers—killed.

Colonial troops eventually persevered, capturing King Philip—hunting him down to Bristol, Rhode Island, then making an example of him by drawing, quartering, and beheading him. Surviving non-Christian natives, for their part, were sold into slavery, human commodity being highly in demand in the growing colonies.

Today, the natives are said to retain their hold of various parts of the Triangle, haunting the land that they were driven from so brutally.

Some claim that Wampanoag chief Anawan lays claim to his namesake rock on Route 44 in Rehoboth; visitors to the area have reported phantom voices speaking in what sound like Native American tongues, the sounds of beating drums, apparitions of blazing fires that emit no heat, smell, or smoke, and the figure of an elderly Native American man (presumably Anawan himself). One theory, according to experts, is that the natives will continue to linger until precious wampum belts that were stolen—and subsequently disappeared—are returned to their rightful owners.

But not only do the natives themselves potentially linger in their usurped spaces, their notorious tormenters are believed to, as well. "Pukwudgies" were legendary in Wampanoag folklore; they were mischievous, elusive troublemakers—short, squat, hairy, and with exaggerated facial features. (Which might explain Russo's encounter?) The Wampanoags eventually came to call them evil, and believed that they had magical powers, such as the ability to disappear and glow in the dark. As some explain, if something went awry, Pukwudgies were considered the culprits.

Visitors to the Triangle have described seeing similar creatures—and at least one member of an investigating paranormal team claimed to be temporarily possessed by one.

Meanwhile, within the Hockomock Swamp, there have been numerous accounts of raptors with twelve-foot wingspans, snakes as thick as stovepipes, red-eyed cats, red-haired orangutans, mountain lions (one so often sighted that it was dubbed the "Mansfield Mystery Cat" and unsuccessfully investigated by police), black panthers, killer dogs that also eluded law enforcement, and, most prominently, Bigfoot.

In the early 1980s, the *Boston Herald* newspaper interviewed a now deceased West Bridgewater resident about his purported brush with one of the world's most infamous, elusive hairy beasts.

"Something was following me and I knew it was big," he was quoted by the story's author, Ed Hayward. "I knew it wasn't a human, because when it passed by me, I could smell it. It smelled like a skunk, musty and dirty, like it lived in the dirt."

"Spook lights" are also a commonly reported phenomenon—various sizes, glowing in many colors (oftentimes changing colors), moving up and down and side to side, seemingly possessing intelligence, even a sense of playfulness.

And of course, no hub of such peculiarities and unknowns would be complete without a few wandering ghosts. Numerous cemeteries in the area are reportedly hangout spots for ethereal, restless beings.

A sinister little boy has made some visitors to Rehoboth's Village Cemetery aware of his presence—naughtily, he asks people to stay and play with him. A mysterious, hovering woman in white has also been seen, as well as a man in dark-colored nineteenth-century attire who is sometimes pounding the ground, wailing and crying. Colonial soldiers and singing women have also been reported at other local burial grounds, and one witness claimed to see a phantom schoolmarm—who disappeared as soon as she appeared—teaching a group of children in one of the area's few remaining historical one-room schoolhouses.

On more of the urban legend side, there have been purported sightings of phantom hitchhikers and antagonistic ghost trucks. But reports in both cases have been spottier, leaving even avid believers dubious.

"The most important thing, especially with ghosts, is a firsthand account," well-known paranormal researcher Jeff Belanger said of the latter tales. "Again and again, you talk to people and they say, 'Oh man, my cousin's brother's former roommate's uncle swears he saw that guy.'"

But even so, the countless other unexplained stories that run rampant around the triangle have made believers out of many.

"The Bridgewater Triangle is real. There's no question in my mind," retired Freetown police lieutenant detective Alan Alves, who investigated the phenomena throughout his career, told the filmmakers of the definitive documentary on the subject. "The weirdest things happen here, the most unexplained things happen here. And you can feel it in that state forest. I dare anybody to go there in the middle of that state forest at midnight, or in the dark, and tell me if you don't sense something that you don't sense anywhere else."

But the mysterious area attracts a far more menacing presence, as well.

Particularly, the 10,000-acre Freetown–Fall River State Forest seems to be host to a disproportionate amount of criminal activity—most of it of the satanic variety.

"It's not a surprise to me that all this crime takes place here, because it's just a darker place," said Weisberg.

In the 1970s, the bodies of at least three women—one of them a known prostitute—were found mutilated. Two were discovered with their hands tied behind their backs and their skulls crushed, prompting local newspapers to assert that their deaths were Satanic offerings. The decomposed corpse of a fifteen-year-old was also discovered tied to a tree, fully clothed.

The sacrifices didn't stop there. Animals of all types have been found all over the forest—pigeons in the center of pentagrams traced in the dirt; mutilated cow carcasses; a dozen baby calves devoid of blood. A pet cemetery had to be shut down due to numerous grave robbings, and the sheer amount of ritualistic activity sparked local police to investigate (to no satisfying end).

Human graves weren't sacred, either. Robbings occurred in remote sections of the forest—and in one of the most notorious cases, a crypt in a mausoleum was broken into at Freetown Cemetery. The perpetrators removed a female body and severed her head. Police recovered the skull tossed in the nearby bushes. The mausoleum is now sealed.

Other instances of the occult have included sightings of people in robes, scattered animal bones, rocks formed into pentagrams, and boulders painted with 666, the infamous "number of the beast." Even more disturbing is the discovery of an abandoned underground bunker and a remote makeshift hut; they were said to be littered with disturbing paraphernalia such as tiny chairs with sadistic bindings, decapitated dolls, tiny figures nailed to trees, assorted graffiti, and upside-down pentagrams.

Ultimately, given all the purported phenomena—from occultists to inexplicable beings to unidentified aircraft—the Triangle is bound to remain a hub of speculation and study (and, for some researchers, awe) for a long time to come.

"When you're looking at the Bridgewater Triangle, nothing can be isolated. All of these things are interconnected," said paranormal researcher Chris Balzano. "For us to ever fully understand what's going on in the Bridgewater Triangle, we have to look at it through a cryptozoological lens. We have to look at it through a ufology lens. We have to look at it through a ghostly lens. Because only when we [have] evaluated the area through all of those different perspectives, and combine our evidence, combine what we've found . . . that's [when] we're ever really going to understand what's going on in the Triangle."

Part 9

VILLAGES OF
THE DAMNED

Some areas just seem to be cursed. Whether because of location or circumstance, untimely placement in history, decidedly more auspicious reasons—or a combination of the above—they dwindle and disappear, inevitably lost to time and memory.

Chapter 35
The Town That Time Forgot

It was said that she was hideously ugly: corpulent, frumpy, possessing two fang-like upper teeth. An old hag with an evil eye and a callous temperament, she made her home—the salacious setting of many fortune-tellings amid copious drams of rum—in a tumble-down clapboard structure at the entrance to a once-propitious settlement on Gloucester's Cape Ann.

Feared and reviled, Tammy Younger was the grand dame among a motley assortment of supposed soothsayers, witches, outcasts, and indigent—those both spurned by society and disdainful of it—who laid claim to a notorious, abandoned north-of-Boston village township known as "Dogtown" that had long been overgrown and forsaken to the elements.

Today, the spot where she once hosted her lewd parties is but a jumble of fallen-down stones taken back by nature; the village where she and her wanton associates practiced their dark arts has devolved and evolved over centuries, now comprising a bramble of trails traversing forests and fields, swamps and bogs.

Yet some believe that the transient spirits of its contentedly vagrant population dwell there still. And a high number of murders and other crimes within its depths over the years—a phenomenon, it should be considered, that can be attributed to many large tracts of uninhabited land—has led some to conclude that the area is eternally damned.

Dogtown is a legendary—and some say cautionary—tale of how time can mutate prosperity into negligence.

Planned around four roads and originally called the Commons Settlement, the village was established in 1693, according to the Essex National Heritage Area, on a high plateau on Cape Ann as a means of protection from the pirates who trolled the outlying harbor and the Atlantic Ocean. Officials measured out a few dozen lots, several families took up residence, and the area flourished with life and activity.

Still, it wasn't long before contentions arose. As Gloucester shifted from agrarianism, growing comparably along with its prospering shipbuilding and fishing trades, residents began to talk of splitting off from the Commons Settlement and establishing separate parishes. Then, as the Revolutionary War began to broil and the state legislature sanctioned pirating along the eastern coast, more and more Gloucester men were shipping off to sea (with many never to experience their long-awaited homecoming). Over the next eight years, as was the case throughout the thirteen colonies, the war was decimating. By the time of the signing of the Treaty of Paris in 1783, Gloucester had lost more than 1,000 residents, or nearly one-fifth of its population, according to Elyssa East, author of *Dogtown: Death and Enchantment in a New England Ghost Town*.

Although many areas eventually recovered, the Commons village, due largely to its high, out-of-the-way location—the prime attraction for its initial siting and settlement, after all—did not. Most of its homes were simply emptied and left to deteriorate as their owners sought more fortuitous work in Gloucester proper and elsewhere.

The area soon became ramshackle and unkempt, its once well-cared-for homes and pathways reclaimed by its lush environs—ivy and weeds clambering about its structures, encroaching trees above its once-wide paths and underbrush below transfiguring them into verdant, narrow tunnels.

This uncultivated and overgrown nature served as a welcoming cloak for the area's destitute and undesirables. Soldiers' widows left impoverished by the war, hobos, drifters, the infirm, and old crones such as Tammy Younger, who flouted their sorceress reputations, migrated up to the largely deserted settlement and squatted in the crumbling dwellings of their choosing. The area was also an asylum of sorts for former and runaway slaves and other misbegotten wanderers.

Soon the nickname Dogtown began to circulate, at first haltingly hushed and whispered, then more hastily slung as a pejorative. According to legend, it originated out of a practice that some considered detrimental for protection: As transients began to encroach, original Commons settlers, many of them widows who couldn't afford to make the exodus south to more desirable areas, started keeping large guard dogs for protection. Over time, as those village foremothers passed, it was said that their canines became homeless, feral, and ran wild throughout the area as it became increasingly more neglected.

However, as East explained, the name was ultimately a common, catchall derogatory term for such disowned locales left to ruin. During the 1800s and early 1900s, there were about sixty different locations, emptied by society's betters and taken over by the downtrodden, with the charged label of "Dogtown" across the United States.

Cape Ann's version came to be known for its gypsy nature, as well as the perversities, backward, and wayward practices that went unbridled within its limits. Its migratory inhabitants made their meager livings through small-scale farming, berry picking, and, most infamously, by engaging in prostitution, reading fortunes, and casting spells. With the area abundant with a literal pharmacy of native herbs and plants, Dogtowners were also said to concoct numerous mystical tonics and potions sought out for their augmentative, healing, intoxicating, and aphrodisiacal qualities.

Meanwhile, in gender-bending, social-mores-flouting practices, women dressed as men and vice versa, with men performing housework and other so-called feminine chores such as washing and nursing, and their female companions taking up such duties as hauling wood and building stone walls.

In more fantastical accounts, the supposed conjurers and enchanters who swarmed the area were said to be seen bewitchingly traversing the sky on brooms—the cliché practice of many a cackling, green-skinned, straw-haired Halloween-night hag. One of those was the brazen "Old Meg," who was also reputed for her transformative qualities. To taunt and intimidate two Gloucester infantrymen who had previously slighted her, she supposedly took on the form of a cackling crow. Flying several miles south from her home in her transmuted form, she swooped and screeched at them, seemingly immune to stone projectiles and bullets. Realizing that this was no earthly bird of prey, the men pulled their silver buttons from their coats, loaded them into their muskets, and fired. The crow was felled and killed—and, dozens of miles away, as the story goes, so was old Meg.

By night, various pirates and sea captains—as well as local men eager for debauchery—ventured within the elastic and slowly expanding borders of the forgotten village to sip on the women's odd brews, hear about their possible futures, and engage in lascivious acts in its so-called red light district. Some of its more well-off and unsuspecting johns, it was said, simply disappeared and were never heard from again (another method by which the freeloading Dogtowners scrounged for money and goods?).

Younger, for her part, hosted many card games and fortune-telling parties flowing with rum and revelry. With her arresting evil eye, it was also said she commanded merchants to provide her with whatever goods she desired. Living at the perimeter of the settlement beside a bridge over a warbling brook, she allegedly flung open the windows of her decrepit abode to squawk obscenities and curses at oxcart drivers daring to attempt passage into or around Dogtown. Should they refuse to leave a token toll of goods or food, the harridan would hex their carts—holding their stunned oxen in place, or simply levitating the cargo she desired right out of their wagons before releasing the terrified drivers from their paralysis and allowing them to speed off.

Even upon her death at age seventy-six, the dreadful old shrew continued to menace. Her casket maker abhorred having her presence in his home, his family refusing to sleep with her coffin in their midst. To finally rid themselves of her earthly body and placate her stormy spirit, members of the surrounding community combined funds to pay for a silverplated coffin.

As both time and the vitality of its derelict residents began to wane, Dogtown's population dwindled, then completely petered out. By 1814, just a half dozen of the original forty-plus homes remained. Feeble and lacking spunk in their advanced age, the lingering inhabitants withered and crumbled along with the structures around them. Some of the final squatters died of exposure; a few of suicide; still others were discovered moribund in dilapidated ruins and carted away by the constable.

The last known inhabitant of Dogtown was Cornelius Finson, or "Black Neil," a former slave who was favored among the witches. As they died off or were deliriously escorted away, Finson remained, living among the undomesticated dogs, boarding himself up in the basement of a tottering old building, spending years fruitlessly rooting and excavating for what he believed was buried treasure. In 1830, he was discovered frostbitten, wrapped in rags and spouting gibberish; the constable took him from the settlement to a poor house, where he died shortly thereafter.

With its miscreant and waylaid occupants mere ghosts among its ruins, Dogtown became ever more dense and untamed; Mother Nature, as they say, abhors a vacuum, and she quickly reclaimed her keep. In 1845, when a work crew was sent to bushwhack the old town paths and pull down what remained of the town's rotting structures, the area was further absorbed back into the wild.

Still, that doesn't mean it has been completely bereft of the listless miscellany of souls who once established a semblance of home within its borders. Over the years, residents and visitors have recalled various unsettling sounds emanating from both nowhere and everywhere: beating drums, the baying and yapping of dogs or werewolves, the unmistakable wail of forlorn women, the murderous hurrahs of pirates, the lurid, whispered entreaties of fortune-tellers. Some have claimed to have felt an evil eye upon them (perhaps that of Tammy Younger?), and still others have reported brushes with beastly, manlike creatures that they could only describe as werewolves.

The area has also continued to attract a sinister and decidedly bizarre element. There have been various high-profile murders and suicides within the Dogtown forest, which is now a 3,600-acre expanse covering much of Cape Ann and preserved by the nonprofit Essex National Heritage Area. Adding a further aura of creepiness and whimsicality to the already intimidating woods, some mischievous hands have placed what some have dubbed a stuffed-animal graveyard—either that or a bizarre art installation. Beanie Babies, teddy bears, baby dolls, hand puppets, and other miscellaneous cloth effigies have been both hung and placed in various parts of the straggling forest—serving as further evidence of the inspiration imbued by abandoned places.

Then there are the perplexing stories of those who for one reason or another, to their detriment, are drawn to Dogtown.

Take retired fisherman James Merry. An aspiring matador, he practiced wrestling with a bull calf that he pastured in a field near the former home of infamous Dogtowner Easter Carter (a healer known for her wiles when it came to herbs and the special boiled-cabbage dinners she put on for local youths). As it grew, however, the bull became ever more difficult for Merry to wrangle. In 1892, his body was discovered gored and smashed upon rocks; a simple stone marker now memorializes him.

Even today, walking within Dogtown's expansive depths can give one a feeling of unease.

Although a trailhead off Reynard Street offers a map, the sprawling area is labyrinthine, not well-marked, and easy to get turned around in.

The first jarring detail is the persistent cadence of gunshots; the woods abut a shooting range, the gunfire sending rhythmic exclamation points through the air.

Passing over gravel that squeaks and squelches beneath sneaker soles, the bisecting trails lead through copses of trees, along a reservoir, sometimes diverting through openings awash with sunlight, other times dead-ending at chainlink fences abutting backyards. Birds caw and serenade one another, bugs whiz about in their busy but aimless way, birches curve overhead like arches, charred scatterings of stones, and disfigured and smashed beer bottles serve as remnants of recent festivities in these old woods.

Down a path several paces are the vestiges of the doomed settlement's one-time center, identified with a rock stamped with "D.T.S.Q." (An abbreviation for Dogtown Square). Diverting tracks run past the remains of cellar holes that are ruinous with time; like a scavenger hunt of sorts, some are easily identifiable immediately in the adjoining woods, others are hidden deep and indiscernible among other random, numerous jumbles and jetties of lichen-covered rocks. Passersby can imagine the shambling shacks that stood here centuries ago, their hosts beckoning with their charms, portents, and potions.

As a sort of Puritanesque antithesis to such anticipated visions of unbridled depravity that once reigned supreme here, a series of several dozen boulders stand stately and pious along one stretch of trail, asserting inspirational and positive messages and advice for good, clean, successful living.

Certainly jarring and out of place for the unsuspecting, they are the design of mid-twentieth-century financial guru, writer, real estate developer, and one-time presidential candidate Roger W. Babson, a Gloucester native. Purchasing 1,150 acres of the former Dogtown woods in 1929, the founder of his namesake private Babson College in Wellesley was able to locate and mark several of the village's former homes, and released one of the first historical pamphlets on the area as a result.

As a means of promoting encouragement and good spirit during the somber tidings of the Great Depression, he hired several unemployed stonecutters to carve sayings into several dozen rocks along what is now the forest's Babson Boulder Trail.

In raised-relief lettering, they proclaim, "Be on Time," "Study," "Work," "Use Your Head," and espouse such virtues as "Initiative," "Integrity," "Intelligence," and "Courage." One of the largest and most imposing, meanwhile, standing at least fifteen feet high, simply declares "Spiritual Power." (We can only assume that this affirmation would set Younger's purported evil eye rolling.)

Sporadic, ranging in size and scope, some situated several paces off the path and others facing away from it, identifying the marked boulders requires a bit of a quest, as well as a few diversionary jaunts. Snug among their midst is the local geographic oddity "Whales Jaw" (or, at least, what remains of it), a giant rock formation that dates to the Pleistocene era. In place for at least 10,000 years, it was given the fitting name—based on Gloucester's maritime heritage and thriving whale-watching tourism—because it resembled the enormous open jaws of a breaching sperm whale. Emblazoned with bits of graffiti that have been scrubbed away by hands and time only to be replaced by the scrawlings of ensuing generations, the characteristic slab succumbed to gravity in 1989 when a big hunk broke off, according to the town.

Ultimately, though, boulders such as Whales Jaw that were shaped by geography, as well as those etched by human hands, stand as a testament to the peculiar quality of this ancient place, a mystique that continues to endure.

Chapter 36
A Woman Scorned

It was a flourishing early seventeenth-century settlement.

Numerous homesteads dotted the Nissitissit River that threaded through its limits. Families were happy, healthy, and productive. Commerce and industry thrummed along its banks and bustling streets: Along with a school, a store, a post office, a tavern and boarding house, the village housed a sawmill, gristmill, carding and clothier mill (which prepared rough fibers for processing, then crafted them into cloth), as well as a blacksmith shop, casket maker, hay rake business, cigar manufacturer, and tobacco market.

But prosperity and vitality were not to last in this charming, teeming little community once known as North Pepperell.

It all changed in one day—when she suddenly dared to appear in town. A mysterious old woman. Odd, esoteric, antisocial, blatantly and unabashedly nonconforming. Some say her surname was Lovejoy—although no one quite knew for sure (or, for that matter, bothered to find out).

Her arrival—and the brutal reception she endured—was said to ensure the imminent and unforgiving demise of the now defunct village of North Pepperell. It has since been absorbed by Pepperell proper, a small community that skirts the New Hampshire border and is just a short thirty-five-minute jaunt from Boston—and holds as one of its most prominent past residents Col. William Prescott, proclaimer of the legendary command, "Don't fire until you see the whites of their eyes" at 1775's Battle of Bunker Hill.

Not long after the Treaty of Ghent and the Battle of New Orleans decisively ended the War of 1812, the strange and unwelcome woman arrived in North Pepperell, disrupting its calm and setting its residents atwitter.

Keeping to herself, not desirous of attention, she moved into an unoccupied cabin along the Nissitissit just a short distance from the town schoolhouse. She then engrossed herself in daily chores such as tending her land and grazing her cows, pigs, and chickens.

All the while, the locals scrutinized her every action (why did she allow her animals to stray so far from her property, disturbing her peace-seeking neighbors?), criticized her appearance (a lilting stoop and a kerchief-covered head), nattered about where she may have come from and why she had so egregiously chosen their town.

She had to have an ulterior motive, they said. She was a witch, they said. Or perhaps just as bad—a Quaker. Both were sins in this strict Puritan environment. In any case, they determined, she was there to mock them, challenge their simple and God-fearing way of life, an apparent agent of the devil or another demon.

So one day, they set to cast her out. As she was unassumingly shambling her way across the town common, she was ambushed. A frail old woman, it didn't take much to overpower her. As she shrieked and thrashed, two town men restrained her while a third set a scorching hot branding iron to the center of her forehead.

When they finally released her, shamed and marred for life by a vile practice typically relegated to animals, it was said that she immediately left town.

But not before she spat bile, spitefully cursing the village.

"In every home," she was said to have howled and screeched, her disfigured forehead running with blood and pus, "the 'death angel' will make his entry in an unusual manner."

Vehemently, she further execrated the town: Fire would consume and destroy all that had been built; the river that now gushed with exuberance would divert its course and the soil would parch; residents, meeting misfortune at every turn, would flee. Within decades, the village would be destroyed.

Once emptying herself of those apocalyptic words, she disappeared—purportedly never to be seen again.

Residents, believing the words to be merely the vitriol of a hateful, damned woman, soon returned to the idyll of their daily lives.

But before long, her portents came to be realized.

Tragedy quickly consumed the town. Massive conflagrations took down homes, mills, and factories—and just as they were rebuilt, they were once again consumed in flames. The town's dam burst, causing the river to lose depth and desiccate. Bizarre calamities befell townspeople—they drowned, vanished, choked, and broke their necks in freakish "accidents." Murders and suicide rates rose, marital discourse was rampant, children became evermore deviant and degenerate.

Eventually townspeople, terrified of what they believed was the witch's curse proven true, began to flee. They neglected homes to ruin, abandoned well-established businesses.

Soon, the village was deserted, left to rot and fester. And its purported plague has been said to permeate its borders;

in ensuing centuries, mystifying fires, murders, and mishaps have continued in the area closest to its confines.

Today, the old village is practically nonexistent, difficult to locate, pockmarked here and there—as is the case with many old New England properties and homesteads—with old stone walls and foundations.

But although it has largely passed into obscurity—remembered by the few fervent students of local history—the old village of North Pepperell stands as a lasting testament to the perils of prejudice and persecution.

Part 10

STRANGE GEOLOGY

Anything that has been touched by our presence—or, it can be assumed, by any being either ethereal or terrestrial, recognized or not—has the capacity to be haunted.

Rocks appear to be such superficial things—plunked down haphazardly in their place by receding glaciers thousands upon thousands of years ago. But for untold millennia, they have served as humankind's guideposts and stepping stones, repositories for our primitive etchings and signatures, building blocks for our civilizations and quizzical entreaties to the skies. They have witnessed and ensured our demise, concealed our treasure, secured some of our greatest secrets and unsolved mysteries—and in some cases, have been diligently guarded by our slighted, weary, restless souls.

Chapter 37

The Elusive Treasure of Dungeon Rock

Painted black and flying no flag, it suddenly appeared and dropped anchor at the mouth of the Saugus River.

Unfamiliar, ominous. A pirate ship.

From within, four huge men emerged, obscured by dark cloaks. They laboriously lowered what appeared to be a large chest into a shallow-bottomed dinghy, then swiftly angled into the current and rowed up the river. Hidden by the gnarled and knobby trees that gathered along the edge of the flowing channel like sentries, the men then set ashore somewhere upstream and disappeared into the thick mantle of the woods.

Their quick, elusive arrival—and most particularly, the supposed loot they were laden down with—quickly became legend, prompting later treasure-seekers, the most prominent of which would die empty-handed following years of obsessive, fruitless searching in an area that would sinisterly (and for fitting reasons) come to be known as "Dungeon Rock."

In the year 1658, in a land still exotic and untamed—threatened by vandals of all types, from natives, to buccaneers, to Vikings, to wild creatures and diseases as yet undiscovered—the Puritan settlers along this lush coastline just north of Boston were doubtless alarmed by the abrupt appearance of the unknown intruders.

Inciting further angst and suspicion, just a few days following their arrival, the men made a foreboding request. At the local ironworks, a note was discovered asking for such implements of torture as shackles, handcuffs, and hatchets, and various items with which to dig. The letter promised that if the requested goods were left at a certain spot, the favor would be returned with a substantial payment of silver. The ironworkers assented, and the pirates kept their word, leaving a bevy of spoils as reimbursement.

And then, at least for a while, the strange men—to the mingled surprise and disquiet of the wary settlers—inexplicably kept to themselves. According to historian Edward Rowe Snow, they chose an area in a deep, narrow valley closed in on two sides and boasting an advantageous vantage point, where they were said to build a small hut, dig a well, and even plant a garden. (In later years the spot would become known, fittingly, as "Pirate's Glen.")

It was a simple, pastoral lifestyle—one they weren't accustomed to, and one that didn't last.

According to Rowe Snow, in short time they were back to their dastardly ways, supposedly taking as a hostage an English royal princess, enslaving and murdering her. (Or this may simply have been a heinous story made up by the British as a reason to strike at the curious invaders.)

Promptly, three of the supposed pirates were captured and shipped to England, where they were later executed. But the fourth, who would come to be known to history as Thomas Veal, escaped. Fleeing into the forest, he eventually established a hideout in a large cave—where it was believed he stashed his sizeable bounty.

After a time, once local and British sentiments mollified over the matter of his flight, Veal found that a domesticated life suited him—he set up a shoemaking business, peddled his wares in Lynn, and was even given a pardon for his past deeds.

Still, he simply couldn't seem to eschew his old habits. In 1685 he became master of a shallop with a crew of more than a dozen men; but before long, he was accused of piracy, engaged in an ensuing harbor battle, then absconded once more for his old sanctuary among the damp, dark caves of Lynn.

Although he ultimately outwitted his pursuers, the elements (as is often the case) inevitably vanquished. In an ensuing earthquake, Veal was trapped as he hunkered in his underground cavern. With his loot as his only remaining ally—or, more accurately, because of the blind alley it had led him to, his ultimate foe—he died suffocating and starving.

It wasn't long before explorers with their imaginations overflowing with doubloons and diamonds came in search of the famed cave—which by now had earned its dire designation as Dungeon Rock.

One of the most dogged in his pursuits was Hiram Marble of the central Massachusetts town of Charlton. A mid-nineteenth-century spiritualist who believed in the dead's ability to communicate with the living, he claimed to have been visited by Veal's ghost. The pirate portended that if Marble went to the rock and dedicated himself to digging, he would be rewarded with the discovery of copious amounts of buried treasure (as well as Veal's long-lost bones).

Without hesitation, Marble obeyed the specter's omen, purchasing five acres of woods near Dungeon Rock to serve as his home while he began his tireless tunneling in 1851, according to Rowe Snow. It was a cumbersome process;

cutting into stone that was described as "very hard por-
phyry" (igneous with coarse crystals), he got a mere 135
feet over the course of twelve years. The man-made tunnel,
seven feet high by seven feet wide, followed a natural cleft
made impassable by the ground-rattling tremor that sealed
Veal in his earthen tomb.

By 1864, Marble, running out of funds, began charging
visitors to see the rock and the passage he had so painstak-
ingly excavated; he also elicited further input from numerous mediums. One of them offered him a long-awaited,
prescient written message from his pirate guide.

"Don't be discouraged," he was to have written through
the medium's hand, according to Rowe Snow. "As to the
course, you are in the right direction, at present. You have
one more curve to make, before you take the course that
leads you to the cave." Alluding to Moses spending forty
years in the desert before finding his way, Veal purportedly
then offered the encouragement: "Cheer up, Marble; we are
with you and doing all we can."

A visit by an unidentified writer that same year—as
recorded by Rowe Snow—described the site's perilous, dingy
conditions. Although their "gray-bearded" guide Marble,
with a "tale of fanaticism" ventured "boldly on with his flickering torch," the writer notes of the experience descending
into the bowels of the tunnel, "we see nothing but somber,
gloomy, dimly-outlined blackness." He went on to recount
a descent down a flight of wooden stairs, groping left and
right through the dark with the "eternal petrification of
earth and fire all around us," as well as the contracting and
expanding nature of the cavern. Passing a pool of murky
water pines, as well as numerous "jagged, overhanging,
jutting, projecting points," the visitor also described walls

smeared with powder and beset with fine-grained drill-holes and the lingering smell of sulfur.

"Whichever way we turn," he concludes, "we discover evidence of the indomitable struggle between man and matter."

Ultimately, it was a struggle that Marble lost; despite his efforts, he never unearthed Veal's treasure. The pirate's prophecy unfulfilled, Marble died in 1868, his body buried in his native Charlton. His son, Edwin, took up the cause, but experienced no more success than his father. After his death in 1880, he was buried beside the rock that had so long vexed his family. For a time, his sister served as guardian of the site, charging twenty-five cents for visitors to view and tour the massive—albeit failed—undertaking.

By the turn of the twentieth century, the fabled rock and the land surrounding it had been absorbed by Lynn Woods Reservation, a now 2,200-acre park flanking Lynn, Lynnfield, and Saugus.

Within the confines of the public space, the boulder sits on an open knoll reached by threading paths; fringed by trees, it rises out of the ground perhaps fifteen feet, exposing chasms and crevasses and narrow channels, passages that require a duck and a stooping crouch to traverse. At its center, an archway with a well-worn path beckons; walk in a few paces—cooler air emanating from within the moist and lichen-covered rock, the encroaching boulder above absorbing the light and casting a dusky pallor over the confined space—turn to the right and face a reinforced iron door. About five feet tall, etched and scribbled and gratified. Yank on it, iron grating on jutting rock, and it gives—but only about a foot; it is chained from the inside. Peek inside and all there is to see is dark and shadow—more rock, wood bracing, a passage that turns off to the right.

Scrambling around it yields numerous damp and cob-webby hollows; spatters of white mildew and indiscernible blue and white graffiti; the detritus of late-night parties.

Hang around long enough—once the birds begin bedding down and the shadows overtake the trees, and you just might catch a glimpse: strange lights, orbs, misty figures traversing the rocks. Veal, watching over his precious treasure to this day? Or Marble, ceaseless in his pursuit of it?

Chapter 38
The Enduring Puzzle of Dighton Rock

Submerged in a riverbed as the water around it swelled and trickled, changed course and carved channels, the forty-ton boulder served as a sort of graffitied signpost for the centuries.

Today, relocated from its centuries-old bed in the rushing Taunton River, the age-ornamented Dighton Rock sits unperturbed and protected inside a small hut in its namesake state park in the small south-of-Boston town of Berkley.

For generations, the nine-and-a-half-foot-wide, eleven-foot-long boulder has baffled archaeologists, scientists, and historians alike, as well as amateur seekers of the obscure and unexplained. It features an overwhelming intaglio of symbols, shapes, initials, curlicues and squiggles, words, figures, crosses, crests, crude animals, and humanoid faces, ranging widely in language, meaning, and age. Likewise, eras layer and overlap one another—up and down, left and right—so that it effectively becomes a jumble of silent voices fighting for recognition.

With thousands of scholarly articles and books dedicated to Dighton Rock (named for one of the small towns sliced through by the Taunton River), theories over the years as to who—or what—created the carvings have varied from the benign to the outright divine.

Some say Jesus; a few point to the devil. Other considerations: aliens, long-traveled survivors of the fabled, sunken antediluvian island of Atlantis, pirates, lost tribesmen of Israel, Egyptians, Romans, Druids, Chinese, unnamed missionaries.

But ultimately, based on archaeological and epigraphical analysis and comparison, as well as examination of hundreds of photographs, paintings, drawings, rubbings and daguerreotypes taken at all times of day and night over the last three hundred years, researchers have come up with a handful of plausible theories.

In 1680, Rev. John Danforth was the first known person to research and copy the rock's various markings. By then it had already gained a certain recognition, according to historian Edward Rowe Snow, with Puritan father Cotton Mather referencing it in his 1690 published sermon, "The Wonderful Works of God Commemorated" (just two years before the fiasco of the Salem witch trials that would make the minister infamous).

Most of the etchings are believed to be the work of natives, what would have likely been the Wampanoag. Danforth identified the rock's peculiar petroglyphs as recounting a battle with men from another country coming down the river in a "wooden house," with corresponding hieroglyphs depicting a shipwreck and a peninsula.

Other etchings on the stone behemoth are said to be the work of Taunton "haymakers"—farmers who trolled up and down the river in the summer and late fall to cut hay, according to Rowe Snow. One inscription, as he describes, dates to 1640 and is simple in substance, appearing to provide directions to a nearby spring of water.

Other carvings are believed to be the work of Phoenicians—an oracle, a butterfly and various gods and goddesses that are meant to represent the past, present and future; Norsemen or Vikings (referencing characters in the legendary Vinland Sagas), and the Portuguese. The latter is a point of contention; researchers dated some inscriptions on the reverse side of the rock—which is much more sparsely adorned—to 1511, claiming that they bear the name of explorer Miguel Corte-Real, as well as his country's V-shaped coat of arms.

A curious and confounding artifact, Dighton Rock's centuries submerged in the Taunton River helped preserve it from the often brutal hands of time and vandals. Embedded in the river bed, it was largely covered at high tide when the water was flowing, burrowed beneath ice when it wasn't. In 1973, as a safeguarding measure during turbulent times, it was moved to its current location and secured behind glass.

Its relevance and validity have waxed and waned as often as the water that once blunted its edges. "It has had the misfortune of being assigned always either too exaggerated or too insignificant a value," Professor Edmund Burke Delabarre of Princeton University wrote in the 1920s.

In either case, its mélange of blanched and dull carvings will continue to serve as subtle echoes of the past—reverberating until they are deciphered, or ultimately lost to time.

Chapter 39

The Tomb of the Unknown Knight

On a suburban side street, amid meticulously green lawns, upscale homes, and the crescendoing whir and hum of passing vehicles, there is a wholly unexpected monument.

At a curve in the road, easy to miss, is an ancient stone carefully encased beneath glass; adjacent to it is a life-sized effigy of a knight in full armor. A plaque between the two commemorates the Scottish "Prince Henry, Earl of Orkney," who is believed to have died in the area on an expedition in 1399, and was memorialized with a rough punch-hole carving set into a local boulder.

Medieval explorers? Here? In this unassuming Metrowest Boston town?

The so-dubbed Westford Knight, a 615-year-old etching, depicts a crude, life-sized portrait of a Scottish nobleman in the full armor of the fourteenth century—although its once crisp lines have long-since been dulled and corroded by centuries of New England weather, neglect, and the unforgiving fingers of time. Adorning a ledge just a half mile or so from Westford's common, it has long been known to townspeople—one of the earliest references was in 1873 in the *Massachusetts Gazetteer*—although for many years, it was attributed as a relic of the natives, believed to depict the figure of a chieftain.

But then in the 1950s, local historian Frank Glynn decided to do some literal and metaphorical digging.

According to *Mysterious New England*, edited by Austin N. Stevens, with the assistance of T. C. Lethbridge of the University Museum of Archaeology and Ethnology in England—who believed that residents of the British Isles made voyages to America long before Leif Ericson and his Norsemen—Glynn identified the Westford knight. A rough rendering made with pointed punches, a flat-headed hammer, and a thick blunt claw, the carving depicts a knight with an open-visored helmet bearing a shield, a knife, a long sword, and scabbard. On the shield are emblems of a star, crescent, brooch, and—in a symbol signifying journey's end—a small boat with furled sails.

As Glynn discovered, it was customary practice in medieval times to mark the spot where a knight fell.

Coinciding with the town's bicentennial, a granite memorial was erected to the fallen nobleman in 1976. It was complemented by the sculpture in 2014, and a glass encasement was also put over the eroding stone to protect it from the further deterioration of acid rain, rock salt, runoff, and other damaging pollutants.

According to the memorial, Prince Henry, First Sinclair of Orkney, was born in Scotland, and "made a voyage of discovery" to North America in 1398, first wintering in Nova Scotia, then sailing to Massachusetts. But "on an inland expedition in 1399 to Prospect Hill to view the surrounding countryside, one of the party died," the plaque reads, and a memorial was literally set in stone.

More than a half millennia later, it continues to serve as a peculiar anomaly, a testament to the fact that history can reveal itself in the most unlikely places.

Chapter 40

The Devil in Ipswich?

The lyrics could just as well go, "The devil went down to Ipswich, he was looking for a soul to steal. . . ."

If you take a walk past the First Church of Ipswich, you can see exactly where Lucifer is said to have left his mark in this small north-of-Boston hamlet. Embedded in the rocks just a few paces from the parish is an oblong, rectangular shape about twelve inches long—said to be a footprint (or, if you prefer, a hoof print).

As the story goes, it dates to the 1740s, when the devil took up residence in a mirror behind the pulpit in what was then Ipswich's Congregational Church, according to Peter Muise in *Legends and Lore of the North Shore*. During meetings and sermons, the diablo himself would peer over the minister's shoulder, concocting temptations.

But after terrorizing locals, he was finally drawn out by the legendary Methodist minister George Whitefield. On a tour from England, he arrived and preached a rousing sermon in the open space across from the church.

Initially, he elicited just a smug response from the devil. But as he accelerated his preaching and the crowd became fervent, the fallen angel burst forth from the mirror and through the church doors and charged the minister, according to Muise. The forces of good and evil were then said to engage in combat, punching and kicking their way up the roof and to the tip of the steeple. It was there that Whitefield was said to fling him away, the devil landing on his foot before bounding away—forever searing the ground with his indelible print.

Part 11

UNEXPLAINED AND UNIDENTIFIED

My mommy always said there were no monsters—no real ones—but there are.
—Newt, James Cameron's *Aliens* (1986)

As long as there have been humans, there have been creatures mocking our stilted dictionary definition of "natural." Mostly they stay hidden: beneath the ocean, inside the forest, within the depths of the darkest places on earth yet beyond discovery. But every once in a while, they emerge. To confuse? To defy? Or to catch a glimpse of us—strange beings ourselves, with our rules and our practices and our whirring minds and machines?

Chapter 41
Dover's "Demon"

Headlights slice a path through a dark spring night on a rural, windy back road. As the Volkswagen—carrying four teenagers, boisterous, chatty, music lightly droning—rounds a corner, its high beams momentarily skim across a section of crumbling stone wall that has been tugged away by time, inertia, and the elements. Tiny skittering creatures, overgrown field grass and ferns, and lichen-covered rocks set in place hundreds of years ago when this area was dominated by pastures, are all illuminated in a sudden flash. The expected backdrop of any rustic road as mid-spring unfurls in New England.

But . . . what was that? Something else there, lurking, watching. Something that doesn't quite fit. No, something that doesn't *at all* fit.

A quick glimpse is enough: Not just sitting or standing on the jumble of stones along this road in pastoral Dover, but literally clinging to them with oversized digits as if desperate to blend in, is a small but humanoid being. Pale and unclothed, measuring no more than four feet long, it crouches on all fours like a dog or a coyote. Its gawky, slipshod body appears frail and weak—a giant, melon-sized head is somehow supported by a gaunt and lanky neck, its movement guided by disproportionately long and gossamer arms and legs.

But the creature's most striking features, perhaps, are its eyes: Large and round, they dominate its face, further diminishing the already indiscernible nose, mouth, and ears to mere specks. And as they behold the passing vehicle, they appear to glow a bright and luminescent orange.

Only one of the car's passengers—along with driver Bill Bartlett—catches a glimpse of the unusual being as the landscape flickers past. But it is enough to leave them alarmed, perplexed, and more than a little curious. Although it takes some convincing from his friends, Bartlett turns around—"bangs a U-ey" in New England speak—to chance another encounter.

Once again, the lights splay over the crumbled section of wall—same rocks gripped by moss, same overgrown weeds, same scampering critters. But it—whatever *it* was, wherever *it* came from—has vanished.

Speeding off, the teenagers marvel that the creature most certainly could not be mistaken for a human, a wayward pet, or even a wild or feral animal local to these parts. "It scared me to death," Bartlett would later tell the Associated Press.

It was just a flicker of a moment under the pall of night, but little could the witnesses know that, as they left the strange being to be engulfed back by the darkness that evening of April 1977, their experience would spur a comprehensive investigation and ultimately spark an enduring legend that continues to permeate nearly forty years later in this small, affluent Boston suburb of roughly 6,000.

The creature the teenagers—as well as a handful of other witnesses, as not just one sighting does a modern legend make—had chanced upon would soon come to be dubbed the "Dover Demon." A malapropos moniker, as it turns out, but one that stuck as quickly as the rumors began circulating.

It was such a strange occurrence for a small upper-class town like Dover, and, as police undertook investigations at a time when the country's interest was already piqued by such explorations of the otherworldly as in *Close Encounters of the Third Kind*, it soon drew attention from national media outlets, as well as the burgeoning paranormal community.

The Associated Press reported that teenagers had seen "a creature resembling comic book conceptions of a spaceman," and that, although it seemed like a hoax, "nagging doubts linger."

Walter Webb, an assistant director of the Hayden Planetarium at Boston's Science Museum who was brought in to investigate, went so far as to call it "one of the most baffling creature episodes ever reported," even though it appeared over just a few days in April 1977 before absconding back to wherever it came from.

In addition to Bartlett and his friends, other witnesses came forward during that eventful spring, corroborating the bizarre being's unusual characteristics.

A few hours after Bartlett's encounter on the same April evening, another teenager, John Baxter, was making his way home a few miles away after a visit with his girlfriend. Suddenly, a figure appeared out of the dark, seeming to beckon to him; he assumed it to be a friend and welcomed the company at the late and desolate hour.

But as they drew closer together, he faltered. This was no human, and certainly not a friend at that. Making out what he could in the shadows, he spied something that he described as monkey-like, standing upright, and possessing a peanut-shaped head. And like Bartlett, he was entranced by a set of eerie glowing orange eyes.

But before he could get any closer—or make out any further details—the animal bolted into a nearby gully. He, in turn, spooked and confused, headed home at a faster clip, not daring to pursue the mysterious creature further.

Although at least one other eyewitness recounted eyes that glowed a phosphorescent green instead of the more frequently reported reddish-yellow hue, the consensus was that the town's abstruse visitor was ultimately something of a hairless, otherworldly lemur: timid, flighty, and wary, alternating between walking upright and on all fours, and possessing enormous, searing eyes, a bulbous head, and a body that appeared hastily assembled of clunky and mismatched parts.

Certainly not what one might expect of a so-called demon. As Cheri Revai notes in *Haunted Massachusetts*, the ultimately benign entity never exhibited any hostile behaviors; instead, it was described as "scurrying away," "creeping skittishly," or appearing "frozen like a deer in headlights."

So the catchy moniker was a misnomer from the start. It was attributed by Loren Coleman, a leader in the obscure field of cryptozoology, the study of animals and creatures whose existence has not yet been proven due to a lack of evidence (think the Loch Ness Monster, or the legendary Bigfoot, both of which have been oft-seen but have left behind scant legitimate clues).

Not a week after the reported sightings, Coleman, from nearby Needham, made a random pit stop in Dover; he had heard of the odd being skulking around town and was immediately (and not surprisingly, given his compunctions) intrigued. He soon teamed up with a handful of other investigators (including Webb), and together they questioned dozens of locals, including friends, family members, and classmates of the purported witnesses.

Ultimately, they came to the determination that the teenagers were "honest and forthright, not known for pranks, hoaxes or other mischief," as described by Joseph A. Citro in *Passing Strange: True Tales of New England Hauntings and Horrors*. Police chief Carl Sheridan agreed, telling the Associated Press that Bartlett was "an outstanding artist and a reliable witness," even though searches by the town's force had turned up nothing.

Bartlett, for his part, sketched out what he could remember in a widely circulated drawing; along with it, he attested that, "I . . . swear on a stack of Bibles that I saw this creature."

Years later, when interviewed by the *Boston Globe*, he steadfastly stood by his testament, vouching that he never made up the story (but admitting that he often wished that he had because of the "embarrassing" attention that has followed him in the ensuing decades). "I definitely saw something. It was definitely weird," he told reporter Mark Sullivan. "I have no idea what it was."

There are a few—although tenuous—theories. Most compellingly, stories of small, elusive, mischievous beings have flourished throughout Native American culture.

The Cree of Canada, for example, long believed in creatures known as "Mennegishi"—who, like Dover's strange guest, possessed big eyes, round heads, long limbs, and essentially invisible facial features, according to Citro. The Penobscots of Maine, meanwhile, passed down legends of two races of humanoid beings who stood about three feet tall and avoided attention because of their repulsive looks.

Then there are the pervasive stories of the short, squat, glowing, prankish Pukwudgies of Wampanoag folklore, and the Makiawisag of Connecticut, who were believed to have the mystical ability of making themselves invisible with a single pointed finger.

Sightings in Dover were largely confined to the oldest part of town—and one that already had at least one instance of unexplained phenomena. Both Bartlett and Baxter's run-ins with the strange creature took place on or near Farm Street, which lies on the outskirts of town and is its second oldest, built on existing Native American trails. Local legend has it that, in the 1600s, one local man encountered the devil on that very stretch of road.

With that in mind, perhaps the "demon" is indeed unique to Dover alone. It may still inhabit its wilds, having developed the clever adroitness to keep out of sight of curious eyes—reveling in its notoriety, but now preferring the peace and tranquility of obscurity.

Chapter 42

Gloucester's Mystery Guest

A beautiful, sunny, early August day—the kind that does not portend at all of the brisk fall biting at its edges.

Along the Gloucester harbor, with a clear view of the roiling Atlantic, two women stroll in gossip as they make their way on an errand. Schooners and other vessels sway with the tide; waves greet dry land with echoing slaps and claps; birds volley in song.

Suddenly, cresting the surface of the water—something big, something strange, an unusual ridge, undulating, leaving a wide and unmistakable wake. Startled and curious, the women shield their eyes and squint for a better look. What is it? Where did it come from?

But almost as brusquely as it appeared, it's gone, leaving just a long furrow of water like a mysterious wisp of its existence. And there among the depths it might have remained—dismissed as a trick of the eye, a play of bright sunlight and reflecting water.

But within days of that August 6, 1817, sighting, the small city of Gloucester—self-proclaimed as "America's Oldest Seaport"—was enchanted with the notion that it was host to its very own mystery of the deep: a sea serpent.

The names of the two women, the purported earliest witnesses of the creature that eventful summer, were not recorded for history—in fact, their story, at first, was tittered at and mocked—but soon enough, dozens of others in the charming city nestled along the sea just north of Boston came forward with their own eyewitness accounts.

Taking up temporary residence in the Gloucester harbor, it was ultimately benign and not at all shy of attention—instead, it appeared to luxuriate in it. The general consensus was that it was dark brown to black in color, measured between seventy and one hundred feet long, and was as thick around as a barrel. Its head was described as flat and pointed, held aloft a foot or more above water, and it resembled that of a sea turtle or a rattlesnake. Some witnesses reported a long protruding tongue at least a foot long, and eyes that were bright and as large as those of an ox.

Fast and flexible, the sea animal had the ability to hold its breath for extended periods, swam an estimated mile every four minutes, and was equipped with jointed vertebrae capable of upward and downward motion (akin to the slither of a caterpillar). It was described as swimming straight forward, playing in circles, investigating boats and, as described by Wayne Soini in his analysis of the case, *Gloucester's Sea Serpent*, acting like a "trained part of the show at SeaWorld," coming across as "the world's most gregarious sea serpent ever."

The reports of the giant swimming beast became such a sensation that the news spread rapidly south—quite remarkably so at a time when the quickest mode of communication was by horse over paths that varied from passable to nearly nonexistent.

Judge John Davis, who headed the Boston-headquartered Linnaean Society of New England, took a particularly keen interest in the case of Gloucester's mysterious visitor. The society, which had been established just three years prior in 1814, was a group of academics dedicated to promoting natural history; it organized meetings, lectures, and excursions, and had amassed its own small museum of artifacts.

Davis, a native of Plymouth, quickly recruited two unpaid volunteers as well as Gloucester resident and political ally Lonson Nash (both men were loyal to the then-faltering Federalist party). Over the next several weeks, Nash himself spied the creature—which he likened to an anaconda—and interviewed various "witnesses" in a strict committee-determined process. As described by Soini, the exact same set of questions was asked of each witness, who were all sequestered and interrogated separately, then required to sign a deposition, review their statement, and swear and sign their name to it before a justice.

Throughout testimony, the creature was repeatedly referred to as "him"—not the more clinical "it"—and August 14, 1817, "still stands as the greatest day of sea serpent sightings on earth," according to Soini. On that one day, New England's version of the Loch Ness Monster was seen by nearly two dozen witnesses (clustered along the shore or hunkered in boats).

Still, although the most well documented, it hasn't been the only mystery of the deep to emerge along Gloucester's rocky and ragged coastline. In 1638, John Josselyn recounted the story of a boat bearing English and Indian travelers who witnessed a "sea serpent, or snake, that lay quoiled [sic] up like a cable upon the rock at Cape Ann." The English, instinctively inclined to shoot it, were dissuaded by their native companions, who—in a testament to the creature's size and strength—warned of certain death if it were not killed outright. In other instances around that time, the unexpected breach of a strange serpent-like beast just offshore was said to stun clam diggers, and an enormous snake seen lurching along the beach terrified all who witnessed it.

There have been even more mystical—and tragic—legends, as well. In one oft-recounted tale, what was described as a woman with the nether parts of a giant fish—complete with fins and a long scaly tail—skimmed through the water, then leapt into a boat full of fishermen. Stunned, one of the seamen grabbed a hatchet and charged the purported mermaid, cutting off her hand as she made her escape. Sinking into the ocean with a sigh, she was never seen again. Others—and this will likely sound familiar to H. P. Lovecraft fans—have described a race of powerful, immortal, fishlike creatures known as "the deep ones" who live in a sunken city off the coast of the North Shore of Massachusetts (their malign nature and habits are described in Lovecraft's *The Shadow over Innsmouth*). They are notoriously evasive of mankind—but vow to rise and destroy us should their habitat be disturbed.

As for the city's legendary serpent of 1817: As the fervor over the creature intensified day by day, at least one trophy hunter chanced an opportunity. On August 14—the record-breaking day of sightings—ship's carpenter Matthew Gaffney drifted within thirty feet of the being, watching it spiral in the water and bare its white underbelly. Raising his gun, he aimed at its head, then shouted victory when he believed he'd hit his mark. But to his shock—and no doubt that of his shipmates as well as onlookers—the serpent reared on the boat, then sunk below it, disappeared, and resurfaced three hundred feet or so away. "I thought he was coming at us," Gaffney recalled to Nash.

By the end of that summer, Nash's report was complete; he sent it, bound and certified, to Davis in Boston, where the Linnaean Society identified the creature's characteristics of size, speed, and flexibility. And the society may very well have gone down in history—instead of obscurity—had it not been for a fateful discovery. In September, a boy walking along Rockport's Loblolly Cove (located on the southern coast of the idyllic seaside town) found and killed an unusual-looking snake: dark, three-feet long, bizarre lumps along its body.

The specimen was soon sent to Boston, where the society reacted with fervent eagerness (despite Nash's misgivings). They published an official report and named a "new species, *Scoliophis atlanticus*" (Latin for "Atlantic humped snake"). Davis also hastily wrote and published a book about the serpent under the Linnaean Society's name.

The "findings" were met with ridicule.

Scientists soon identified the "specimen" as a common black snake that had somehow become deformed. Not long after, the committee ceased its examination. By 1822, just eight years after its inception, the group voted to suspend its meetings and was soon disbanded.

Along with the discrediting, the serpent itself seems to have soon taken its leave, as if sensing its fading relevance. Reports in Gloucester dwindled to a din and then ultimately ceased. In the ensuing decades, scattered reports of a similar creature echoed sporadically up and down the North Shore—from Lynn, to Manchester-by-the-Sea, to Newburyport (with one final gasp in July of 1960 in the famed fishing city where it made so many headlines 140 years prior). Some speculated that it died off or tired of the two-legged landlubbers it initially seemed to romp and preen for. Others believe that it was forced farther out to sea as a result of overfishing along the coast.

Could it be that Gloucester, whose residents have relied for centuries on the sea for their livelihood and prosperity, is a lure for the mysterious beings that potentially lurk beneath the depths of the vast and unfathomable Atlantic? Or are such sightings and experiences to be expected in a maritime setting so thoroughly enraptured with the water that hugs its shores?

Until—or if—the so-called serpent breaches the surface again, it will remain another of the ocean's many mysteries.

Chapter 43
UFOs over Boston

As a TV reporter charged with practicing impartiality and an innate skeptic, Steve Sbraccia honestly believed that people who claimed close encounters with unidentified objects (from outer space or otherwise) were publicity hounds or had something seriously askew in their heads.

Until that night out on Route 106.

Driving unassumingly along the rural byway south of Boston, he looked up to see a giant, illuminated object. Something completely unusual, something that he could never—not to this day—explain. Diamond shaped—or, as any fervent New England baseball fan might describe it, resembling home plate—it spanned the width of five 747s flying tip to tip.

Briefly, it hovered. Then, with a gust, it took off, blotting out the stars and the inky-black sky in the unmistakable shape of an arrow as it passed overhead and disappeared into the dark depths of the night.

"Up to that point, I had been 100 percent skeptic," Sbraccia recalled in the 2013 documentary *The Bridgewater Triangle* by filmmakers Aaron Cadieux and Manny Famolare. And while the experience didn't transform him into a full-fledged, card-carrying ufologist, he acknowledged that it did crack open the door in his brain that allows in such otherworldy possibilities.

UFOs might just as easily be called "ubiquitous flying objects." Visit any corner of the globe, and if you ask around enough, you're bound to hear stories of unusual lights, aircraft, and entities occupying the void above. And it's no different in Boston and its environs. Since long before European settlers first came aground on the shores of New England's wilds, there have been stories of odd and potentially alien beings traversing the night skies.

One of the first recorded sightings in the Boston area was set down in 1638, not twenty years after the Pilgrims took their first fateful, precipitous steps onto the untamed shores of Plymouth. James Everell and two friends were rowing along the Muddy River—which now runs through Boston's Emerald Necklace Conservatory—when a bright, fiery square of light materialized before them. Willowy and shape shifting, it took on the form of a swine, then moved "swift as an arrow" before it finally disappeared, as retold by Cheri Revai in *Haunted Massachusetts: Ghosts and Strange Phenomena of the Bay State*.

Later, the men reported a condition common to purported UFO eyewitnesses: the unmistakable feeling of lost time. After the shock began to dull, the trio realized they were at least a mile up the river from where they had first set their craft in—but with memories as foggy as the night, they had no recollection whatsoever of paddling the distance. Ultimately, because they were prudent and well respected—and they lived in a time when superstitions and otherworldly phenomena were, if not wholeheartedly accepted, more roundly received and in some cases heeded— their story was believed. Puritan leader and Massachusetts Bay Colony governor John Winthrop even made note of the strange run-in for history's sake in his account of notable New England happenings from 1630 to 1639.

Many other early reports—perhaps due to the fact that they predate the science of meteorology by centuries—are more ethereal and mystical than more contemporary sightings of enormous, iridescent flying discs or, as Fox Mulder (David Duchovny) characterized them in the cult 1990s TV show *The X-Files*: "little green men."

In August 1765, for example, witnesses were captivated and alarmed by a "flying black giant" approximating the size and shape of a human body, as documented in the *Boston Gazette*, one of the first pre-Revolutionary War newspapers. Hovering over Boston, it remained until sunset, and "thousands saw it," author Patricia Hughes recounted in *More Lost Loot: Ghostly New England Treasure Tales*.

Locals watched as the entity touched down, alighted, flopped, and swelled. Floating about twenty feet off the ground, it let forth vapor smoke and sparks, grew "excessively black and fierce," and boomed thunder that tore down at least one building and "shook the lofty fabric and all the little houses, and hollow hearts did hear it." After more than four hours of this relentless, ferocious behavior, it suddenly vanished, leaving behind an abrupt tranquility and silence.

A similar oddity was reported traversing the northern Massachusetts coast more than a dozen years later. In April 1778, scores of witnesses spanning the southern tip of New Hampshire down the contours of the shoreline to Boston watched astounded as a peculiar black cloud strode a few feet above the ground, moving at the speed of a galloping horse. Passing unperturbed through walls and fences "as one goes through water," it set forth the continual shriek of "Hoo! Hoo!" as described by Hughes.

Out of shock and fear, some women looking on helplessly fainted.

Meanwhile, in a more bizarre—and ultimately grotesque—occurrence in 1846, what was characterized as a "luminous flying disc" spewed down a "fetid-smelling jelly" onto the prosperous mill city of Lowell a half hour northwest of Boston. The rancid mass was later purportedly collected and was found to weigh more than 440 pounds and measure roughly four feet in diameter.

Not surprisingly, in recent years following the enduring mystery of Roswell, New Mexico, and the proliferation of post-nuclear era pop culture phenomena that embrace the unknown and obscure, such unexplained encounters have only accelerated.

The mid- to late twentieth century was plentiful with stories of mysterious visitors in the skies.

Above the Boston suburb of Bedford: a sphere, pulsating red and white.

Highlighted against the dark in nearby Woburn: a color-changing streak.

In the sleepy town of North Wilmington: a bright, grapefruit-sized object.

Elsewhere in the region: round projectiles that zipped up and down and around and changed color as fast as they alighted and withdrew.

Astonished viewers, heads tilted skyward, snapped Polaroids that were then widely circulated by the media and, in a few cases, even investigated. For instance, in one well-publicized case in the early 1950s, a seaman posted with the Salem Coast Guard witnessed what he related as a quartet of bright lights alternately brightening and dimming—almost, as it were, attempting at a signal. The Coast Guard mulled over the odd story for a decade, eventually reporting perplexedly of the incident that "it has never been determined what caused the phenomenal lights." Another case from 1966 remains similarly unsettled. In the North Shore town of Beverly, witness descriptions corroborated the appearance of a bright, football-shaped bulk up above; as big as a car, it made a whizzing sound like something out of an Ed Wood movie and recurrently flashed a series of primary colors. Onlookers purportedly watched it land on the field adjacent to the high school before hovering momentarily over the building and then taking off.

The widely reported encounter soon became notorious; it was eventually investigated by the Condon Committee (part of the University of Colorado UFO project). Their analysis found that, although the circumstance "did not yield impressive residual evidence" to support the hypothesis of an alien object, it could "fit no other explanation if the testimony of the witnesses is taken at full value."

Over the years, reports of unexplained run-ins continued to filter into police stations and media outlets. Various headlines blared: "Mysterious Balloon over Bridgewater!" "UFOs over Randolph? Some Persons Say Yes!"

Accounts have ranged from detailed to ambiguous, describing presences from overwhelming to mere pinpoints, detailing run-ins both fleeting and excruciatingly long-lasting, at a distance or disturbingly up close.

Visit any number of websites, and you'll read about— and in some cases view attempts at pictorial evidence—a spectrum of confrontations logged in and around Boston. They range from white beams emanating from no discernible point, to floating lights shining and blinking any manner of colors known to humankind (and some decidedly not), to hovering craft infinitesimal, immense, round, square, triangular or torpedo shaped, to orbs of all sizes and colors dancing, circling, vibrating—acting both playful and ominous, seemingly sentient and aimless.

Could they ultimately *be* otherworldly or alien? A product of human imagination or undercover innovation? A trick of the eye, atmospheric gasses—or (as could be the case with Bigfoot, the "demon" of Dover, and a bevy of roaming sea monsters) some as-yet undiscovered terrestrial being?

Especially now with the Mars rover trundling across the red planet, Voyager 1 passing into interstellar space, and numerous other probes exploring the unknown and uncharted (at least by humans) depths of the solar system, the skies above will continue to captivate and allure us. Whether or not they ever give up their secrets, we will always look up—as we have since our simian ancestors roamed the earth—to reflect on and contemplate the unknown.

And in some cases, maybe even make contact.

Part 12

HISTORY EXPLORED

The more enlightened our houses are, the more their walls ooze ghosts.

—Italo Calvino

And quite enlightened is the Old Manse in Concord.

Dating to the mid-eighteenth century and home and host to the likes of Nathaniel Hawthorne, Henry David Thoreau, and the cerebral Alcott family, it—as well as its bevy of visitors both alive and ascended well beyond the confines of this earth—has stood watch as humans have died, lived, withered, prospered, formed ideas and revolutions, scrapped them, regressed, and progressed.

Chapter 44

An Evening at Concord's Historic Old Manse

The steep, narrow set of stairs objects with creaky whines. Flashlights slice through the darkness, bouncing, darting, sweeping, revealing glimpses of the unknown surroundings in strobe-like fashion.

The group, composed of those claiming to possess a variety of sensitivities to the world—or worlds—beyond our sentient one, slowly enters the attic, a warren of brick passages and alcoves.

At the landing, they split; three or four this way, a half dozen or so in the other direction. One group files to the end of the sparse alley, their lights grazing across the walls, beams catching shifting shadows and flecks of centuries of lazy, roused-up dirt particles. They pass one niche housing dozens of chamber pots; in another, flowered wallpaper, grimed and dingy with age, is unfurling itself in large sections from the wall.

All the way to the back and to the left, a small room; they enter, gather in a circle, their array of tools for investigating the paranormal casting an ethereal red glow on the hewn floor.

Scantily furnished with just a bed, the tiny chamber in the "wild and uncivilized" garret (as one-time resident Nathaniel Hawthorne bluntly described it) of the Old Manse in Concord, was once a lodging room for aspiring ministers. "Holy men," as Hawthorne wrote in his 1854 memoir of the property, "in their youth, had slept, and studied, and prayed there."

On this summer evening, it is stiflingly hot, musty with ages, the bodies cramped into the tight space contributing to the shroud of claustrophobia.

Ron Kolek, founder of the New England Ghost Project, the Massachusetts-based paranormal investigation team leading the group tonight of this well-known haven of ghosts, asks for a volunteer. Reluctantly, one comes forward; his chilling duty is to stand within the narrow confines of the room's only closet—door latched closed—while the researchers attempt to coax out one of the shy spirits that are believed to spend their afterlife within these walls.

"Are there any ministers here?" Kolek asks of the room, outfitted with just the necessities of a bedpan, clothes hanging rack, two mirrors, and a small fireplace.

His fellow investigators are equipped with an infrared camera, temperature gauges and electromagnetic field (EMF) readers (used to read fluctuations that could indicate a spectral presence), a device that records electronic voice phenomena (EVP, or sounds or voices of unknown origin), and pendulums and L-shaped dowsing rods (both subjective to each user, pattern of swings and movement determining answers to asked questions).

"A simple sign would work," continues Kolek, a tall, soft-spoken sexagenarian dressed simply in a T-shirt, jeans, and baseball cap. "If you can move something—not much."

Nothing. Just hushed breathing. A small window reveals white pine trees in dusky silhouette. An owl hoots somewhere on the historic property dating to the mid-1700s.

Then suddenly: A series of unmistakable knocks from the closet—and the door leading out to the attic's alley creaks open several inches, hinges rustily screeching.

"You're not trying to get out, are you?" Kolek asks of the cloistered volunteer.

"That's not me kicking the door."

"You're not leaning against the door?"

"I'm not leaning against the door."

The pendulums begin swinging in more and more vigorous circles and arcs; the dousing rods pivot back and forth like antennae. Those sitting closest to the exit door feel a chill, curling their shoulders up defensively to their necks as if expecting a hand to reach out of that black void for a light caress.

Kolek continues, gentle in his enticement. "We're really curious about you, and we'd like to speak with you."

The EVP device begins to crackle. Distorted voices form words: "Careful." "Simple."

"These people came a long way to meet you, to visit you," Kolek volleys, "to try to understand why you're here."

"Correct."

"Is there more than one spirit here tonight?"

"Pupil."

"Would you like to learn from us?" "Are we your pupils?"

A different volunteer, this time female, takes a place in the closet—also known as the "sermon room," because it was where the ministers-in-training practiced reciting them. As the group continues its line of questioning, she reports a slow audible rapping inside, as well as a distinct temperature drop.

To enhance the supposed communication link, Kolek takes out a "spirit box." Also known by the nickname "shack

hack"—hearkening to the days when Radio Shack was the dominant force in electronics—it's a modified AM/FM radio that constantly and speedily scans up and down the dial, a process that purportedly enables spirit voices to more easily cross the divide.

"What is your name?" Kolek queries.

Several voices "reply" as the box tremolos up and down the channels like hands running along the length of piano keys.

"Luther." "Mercy." "Stop."

"What are you trying to tell us?"

Indecipherable voices fade in and out; feedback squawks.

"Do you want us to leave?"

"Uh-huh."

The other members of the team begin to join in with a volley of queries: "Open the door for us." "How about just rattle the door?" "Can you just make a noise?"

One voice, ominous and final, replies: "Leave."

Then the room falls silent. That's apparently all the supposed ghosts—whoever they are, whenever they lived here—wish to reveal tonight.

ALIVE WITH GHOSTS—AND HISTORY

The Old Manse is one of the many historically gilded buildings in Concord—and also believed to be one of the most haunted in a city where history is, quite literally, glimpsed at every turn.

Most renowned for its role in the American Revolution—its Old North Bridge was the site of one of the opening battles of the American Revolution, in those initial days referred to as the American War of Independence—Concord was also known as the "American Athens" because of the fertile transcendentalist minds who congregated there in the 1800s.

Built in 1770—although it's not known whether it was constructed from the ground up or remodeled out of an existing building, according to author Paul Brooks— the Olde Manse, a buttercream-colored, Georgian clapboard building, sits on nine acres overlooking the Concord River and a replica of the Old North Bridge. On April 19, 1775, still a relative infant when it comes to the lives of buildings, it stood as a silent spectator to the fateful Battle of Concord.

The nonprofit Trustees of Reservations purchased the property in 1939; located just off Monument Street, through a gate down a path bordered with trees, it is listed on the National Register of Historic Places, and is a popular tourist destination. Two-hundred-forty years ago, it was built for William Emerson, Ralph Waldo Emerson's grandfather, pastor of the Church of Concord, according to Brooks's *The Old Manse and the People Who Lived There*. He was succeeded by Ezra Ripley, who boarded Ralph Waldo Emerson for a year in 1834—a year the thirty-two-year-old poet and essayist spent writing his first book, *Nature*, which essentially served as the foundation for transcendentalism, a philosophical movement based on the belief that people are inherently good but are easily corruptible by society and institutions.

Not ten years later, in 1842, the young, Salem-born writer Nathaniel Hawthorne moved in with his new bride, Sophia. The newlyweds spent three years there, a period in which Hawthorne wrote some of his most famous short stories, including "The Celestial Railroad" and "Rappaccini's Daughter," but before he set down the works that would make him an American icon, *The Scarlet Letter* and *The House of the Seven Gables*. During his tenure, he welcomed the greatest minds of the time, such as Emerson, Henry David Thoreau (who would publish his renowned *Walden* in another ten years' time), pioneering teacher and philosopher Bronson Alcott, Margaret Fuller, an Emerson protégé, journalist, and women's rights advocate, and poet William Ellery Channing.

Ever the romantics, Hawthorne and his wife used a diamond ring to etch simple pronouncements onto windowpanes: "The smallest twig leans clear against the sky," "Man's accidents are God's purposes," "Inscribed by my husband at sunset, April 3, 1843. On the gold light."

The literary couple, along with several of their transcendentalist compatriots, is buried not far away in an area known as "Author's Ridge" in the Sleepy Hollow Cemetery (sharing a name with the one in New York State famous for its headless dead resident).

When Hawthorne returned to his home city of Salem, the property was passed to Samuel Ripley (son of the aforementioned Ezra) and his wife Sarah, who lived there for twenty years after her husband's sudden death. Three generations of their descendants—the notable Emerson-Ripley family—then lived there until the property was set aside as a landmark.

Well-regarded mural painter Edward Simmons, Sarah Ripley's grandson, wrote of his memories of the Manse in his 1922 autobiography. In an ode that endures ninety-five years later, he summed up its legacy: "The Concord literati are gone, the town has completely changed, but the Old Manse is still there, holding many secrets."

Among those: its numerous residents and visitors of the phantom variety.

Hawthorne was the first to note their presence.

"Houses of any antiquity, in New England, are so invariably possessed with spirits, that the matter seems hardly worth alluding to," the burgeoning author wrote in his 1854 *Mosses from an Old Manse*, a tribute to his years living on the historical property.

"Our ghost," as he described, would "heave deep sighs" in the parlor, rifle through paper "as if he were turning over a sermon" in the upper entry, but was nevertheless invisible, "in spite of the bright moonshine that fell through the eastern window." Hawthorne also described him as sweeping through the midst of a discoursing company one evening at twilight, "so closely as almost to brush against the chairs," but was still covert, only identified by the distinct rustle of his silk minister's gown.

After visiting the attic, an area the novelist described as beset with "nooks, or rather caverns of deep obscurity, the secrets of which I never learned, being too reverent of their dust and cobwebs," he surmised that the ghost was a pastor of the Concord parish more than a century before, a contemporary of Anglican preacher George Whitefield. (He was most likely referring to Rev. Daniel Bliss, according to the records of the First Parish in Concord, who held outdoor mass meetings and was, as Hawthorne noted, of "fervid eloquence.") He came upon Bliss's visage, in a wig, band, gown, holding a Bible, on a roll of canvas in the "Saints' Chamber."

But Bliss wasn't alone; there was apparently also the boisterous ghost of a servant maid who would clank and bang around in the kitchen "at deepest midnight," cooking, ironing, grinding coffee—although there would be no evidence of these tasks being done the following morning, according to Hawthorne.

"Some neglected duty of her servitude . . . disturbed the poor damsel in her grave, and kept her at work without any wages," he wrote.

Hawthorne's ghosts have been joined by an assembly of others over the years. Many visitors, staff, and passersby have reported a woman in Victorian dress sitting in one of the Manse's many front windows.

In other instances, shadowy figures have sauntered upstairs or into the downstairs parlor, only to inexplicably disappear—such a distressing experience that some interpreters purportedly refuse to go inside the structure after dark, according to Kolek. Numerous eerie raps and taps have been heard throughout the building, as well, and books have alighted off shelves and flown across rooms at guests. In the attic, where Hawthorne came upon the painted likeness of his benevolent ghost, meanwhile (and in a moment that sounds like a scene straight out of a demon-riddled James Wan movie), a vintage baby carriage creakily rolled several feet across the floor, Kolek said—no detectable hands anywhere nearby, no discernible draft, and the old-fashioned covered stroller rolled *up* a slight pitch in the floor, so no attributing the occurrence to gravity.

During a recent investigation on a late-summer night, there were several other believed spectral encounters.

A group of about two dozen gathered to explore the eighteenth-century property—the curious, the keen, those who claimed to have otherworldly perceptions and sensitivities. In addition to the experience in the attic, those who explored the front parlor claimed to interact with the apparition of a fourteen-year-old boy who had suffered head trauma; someone in that same room also had the sensation of their arm being touched by unseen hands.

ENDINGS UNCLEAR

A little before midnight, the group walks single file from a "base camp" conference-space area at the back of the building through a washroom and kitchen, down a narrow hallway lined with portraits and bookcases, and decorated with cream-colored French-drapery trompe l'oeil wallpaper. Up an equally confining staircase—with a spookily coincidental thirteen steps—they then enter a room at the far right (from the outside, looking up: the left second-floor bedroom).

Pendulums swaying, dowsing rods rotating, the illumination from the various instruments casting over-exaggerated, Nosferatu-like shadows on the walls, they ask a string of inquiries of the dark space.

"Is there more than one spirit energy with us?"

"Do you want to communicate with us?"

The answers, according to the movement of the devices, are all "yes," although the alleged apparitions here seem to be shy or wary. One member of the group with avowed acuteness of the unknown claims to sense them and describes them as "pacing around, checking everyone out."

Adding to the ghoulish atmosphere: A frilly, wedding-white dress—belonging to the Victorian lady witnessed by so many in the window?—drapes the bed, as if awaiting a wearer soon to appear. Fertile minds can only imagine it billowing with life and arising to greet its flesh-and-blood visitors.

Soon, the researchers depart the room and its phantoms, offering the pleasantries "We appreciate it very much," and "Nice meeting you."

The night's final destination: Old North Bridge. Amid the croaking of frogs and the cheeping of crickets, the crew makes the short walk down to the river just around midnight, traversing a dewy field beset by fruit trees and a giant boulder where Thoreau was said to sit and ruminate, passing along a crunching gravel path.

At least two in the group pick up on a lingering sense of agony once they reach an obelisk monument beside the grave of British soldiers (the resting place of two redcoats, according to the National Park Service).

"I feel death and fear and transition," one remarks. Another, breathing heavy, bent over, declares, "No one's happy here. No one's happy right now."

On the arched wooden footbridge—a replica erected in 1956 and restored in 2005, according to the National Park Service, the fifth built on-site over the last 240 years since the original was taken down in 1788—the spirit box is again employed. Its bluster of static and shrill feedback clashes with the placid nature of the subtly meandering river, the mist floating in its shiftless way, the splay of stars overhead.

"Can you say hello?" Kolek asks.

His entreaty is merely met with crackles and squeals.

Another question: "How many British soldiers are here with us now?"

After a pause, the faint, contradictory replies of two distinct voices: "Forty-six." "Seventy-nine."

"Are there minutemen here—and if so, can you give us a really clear number?"

No answer for that query; instead, the simple but portentous: "They . . . knew . . ."

There is a volley of additional inquiries, but the spirit box bears nothing conclusive; apparently the brief exchange is all the shades lingering here could muster.

Kolek finishes with a solemn "Thank you"—which is met by a very audible and clear "You're welcome."

After a solemn walk back up to the building, the group departs, car lights splashing arcs over hundred-year-old stone walls and against even more aged trees.

The Manse once again sits dark at the end of its tree-lined lane, its windows lidless eyes, its double chimneys and attic gable the only protuberances from its boxy silhouette.

But . . . what was that? A sudden flicker, a refraction or reflection behind one of the panes—just the imagination? Or one of its eternal residents bidding adieu?

APPENDIX A: SEEKING OUT BEANTOWN'S HAUNTS

Beyond the requisite attractions—Faneuil Hall, Fenway Park, the Bull and Finch Pub that inspired the incomparable 80s sitcom *Cheers*—Boston and its surroundings allure with their assembly of ghosts, ghouls, and creepy, possessed, and haunted locations.

No list can ever be 100 percent comprehensive—and some sites mentioned in this book had to be left out because they, in turn, have been omitted by time—but these are the chilling essentials.

So explore . . . they're just dying to see you. . . .

CEMETERIES WITH A CREEP FACTOR

Central Burying Ground
On Boylston Street side of the Boston Common
139 Tremont St., Boston, MA 02116
Open daily 9 a.m. to 5 p.m.

Copp's Hill Burying Ground
45 Hull St., Boston, MA 02113
Open daily 9 a.m. to 5 p.m.

Danvers State Hospital Cemetery
Located in the woods below Halstead Danvers
1101 Kirkbride Dr., Danvers, MA 01923

Park at the memorial and follow a dirt path directly to the left behind the newest construction.

Forest Hills Cemetery

95 Forest Hills Ave., Boston, MA 02130
Gates open at 7 a.m.; closing hours change with the seasons.
Call (617) 524-0128.
foresthillscemetery.com

Granary Burying Ground

Tremont Street, Boston, MA 02108
Open daily 9 a.m. to 5 p.m.

King's Chapel Burying Ground

58 Tremont St., Boston, MA 02108
Open daily 9 a.m. to 5 p.m.

Lowell Cemetery

77 Knapp Ave., Lowell, MA 01852
Lowell Street and Knapp Avenue gates are open 8 a.m. to 8 p.m. in the spring and summer; 8 a.m.to 4 p.m. in the fall and winter. Call (978) 454-5191.
lowellcemetery.com

Mount Auburn Cemetery

580 Mount Auburn St., Cambridge, MA 02138
Gates open 8 a.m. to 6 p.m., varying with the season. The Washington Tower closes an hour before the gates. Call (617) 547-7105.
mountauburn.org

Old North Church Underground Crypts
193 Salem St., Boston, MA 02113
Visit by paid tour only, $6 for adults, $5 for students/seniors/military, $4 for children under 12. Tours are on weekends and run hourly from 10 a.m. to 3 p.m. (except from noon to 1 p.m.) in March; hourly from 10 a.m. to 4 p.m. (except during the noon hour) in April, May, November, and December; every half hour from 10 a.m. to 4 p.m. (except at noon and 12:30 p.m.) from June to October; tours are by special appointment only in January and February. Call (617) 858-8231.
oldnorth.com/btstours

Pine Ridge Pet Cemetery
238 Pine St., Dedham, MA 02026
Hours 9 a.m. to 3:30 p.m. Call (617) 226-5652.
arlboston.org/pine-ridge-pet-cemetery

LURID LOCALES
The Boston Common
139 Tremont Street, Boston, MA 02116

The Bridgewater Triangle
There are many spooky and notorious locations to be seen here. Start by exploring the lush Hockomock Swamp, beginning at Lake Nippenicket, just west of Route 24 off Route 495 in Bridgewater. Also check out the Freetown–Fall River State Forest, 110 Slab Bridge Rd., Assonet, MA 02702.
Visit thebridgewatertriangledocumentary.com for more ideas.

Dogtown
Cherry Street, Rockport, MA 01966
Follow Route 128 in Gloucester to Grant Circle Rotary. Follow exit toward Lanesville, Route 127, take a right onto Poplar Street, then left onto Cherry Street. Dogtown Road parking area will be about a mile on the right.
Open dawn to dusk. Pick up a trail map at the trail head.

Fort Independence on Castle Island
2010 William Day Blvd., South Boston, MA 02127
Open only to one-hour free guided tours, noon to 3:30 p.m., Memorial Day weekend through Columbus Day weekend. Twilight viewings on Thursday evening in the summer. Call the Castle Island Association at (617) 268-8870.
www.bostonfortindependence.com

Fort Warren on George's Island
Accessible by the Boston Harbor Islands ferry from May to October. Call (617) 223-8666.
bostonharborislands.org

Salem
The Witch City is filled with legends, lore, and just pure history. Start at the Salem Visitor Center at 2 New Liberty St., Salem, MA 01970. Also visit salem.org and salemweb.com/guide/tour.

SITES SURE TO GIVE YOU CHILLS
The Boston Athenaeum
10½ Beacon St., Boston, MA 02108
First floor and exhibition galleries are open to the public from 9 a.m. to 8 p.m. Monday through Thursday; 9 a.m. to 5:30 p.m. Friday; 9 a.m. to 4 p.m. Saturday; and noon to 4 p.m. Sunday. Call (617) 227-0270.

Boston Light
Little Brewster Island, Boston Harbor
Accessible by a three-and-a-half-hour ferry tour that departs daily on Friday, Saturday, and Sunday between July 5 and October 4. Pick up the ferry at the Boston Harbor Islands Welcome Center on the Rose Kennedy Greenway.

Dighton Rock
Located inside a pavilion in Dighton Rock State Park, Bay View Avenue, Berkley, MA 02779
Off Route 24, follow exit 10, go west two miles and follow signs to the museum.

Dungeon Rock
On Dungeon Road inside Lynn Woods Reservation, Pennybrook Road, Lynn, MA 01905

Hammond Castle
80 Hesperus Ave., Gloucester, MA 01930
Open seasonally
(978) 283-2080
hammondcastle.org

Holden Chapel
1350 Massachusetts Ave., Cambridge, MA 02138
Located in Harvard Yard on the Harvard University campus

Huntington Theatre
264 Huntington Ave., Boston, MA 02115
(617) 266-7900
huntingtontheatre.org

Ipswich Devil Imprint

Located on a rock—encircled in spray paint—in front of First Church, UCC, at 12 Meetinghouse Green, Ipswich, MA 01938.

Lizzie Borden Bed and Breakfast Museum

230 2nd St., Fall River, MA 02721
Tours every hour from 11 a.m. to 3 p.m., seven days a week, year-round. Adults $18, seniors $15, children ages 7 to 12 $10, children under 6 free. Want to stay? Two-person room rate packages begin at $200.
(508) 675-7333
lizzie-borden.com

The Olde Manse

269 Monument St., Concord, MA 01742
Free; hours vary with the season. Call (978) 369-3909.
thetrustees.org/places-to-visit/greater-boston/old-manse
.html

The Omni Parker Hotel

60 School St, Boston, MA 02108
(617) 227-8600
omnihotels.com/hotels/boston-parker-house

Tewksbury State Hospital / Public Health Museum

365 East St., Tewksbury, MA 01876
Open Wednesday, Thursday, and first Saturday of the month, 10 a.m. to 2 p.m., and by special tour. Museum admission is $5, walking tour is $10.
(978) 851-7321 ext. 2606
publichealthmuseum.org

The Veasey Estate / Veasey Memorial Park
201 Washington St., Groveland, MA 01834
(978) 521-9345
veaseypark.org

MACABRE MONUMENTS
Black Dahlia Memorial
Salem Street, Medford, MA 02155
Stone plaque sits next to the I-93 rotary.

Myles Standish Gravesite
Inside the Myles Standish Burial Ground, Chestnut Street, Duxbury, MA 02332

Pierce Tomb, Newburyport
Inside Old Hill Burying Hill, adjacent to the Bartlett Mall, Newburyport, MA 01950
The Gothic triangular tomb is at the crest of a hill toward the middle of the cemetery.

The Westford Knight
Located alongside Depot Street (a few hundred yards before Abbot Elementary School, 25 Depot St.), Westford, MA 01886

APPENDIX B: SOURCES

BOOKS

Austin, William. *Peter Rugg, The Missing Man*, 1882. (Via Google Books)

Baltrusis, Sam. *Ghosts of Boston: Haunts of the Hub.* Haunted America. Charleston, SC: History Press, 2012.

———. *Ghosts of Cambridge: Haunts of Harvard Square and Beyond.* Haunted America. Charleston, SC: History Press, 2013.

———. *Ghosts of Salem: Haunts of the Witch City.* Haunted America. Charleston, SC: History Press, 2014.

Belanger, Jeff. *Weird Massachusetts: Your Travel Guide to Massachusetts' Local Legends and Best Kept Secrets.* New York: Sterling, 2008.

Bridgman, Thomas. *Epitaphs from the Copp's Hill Burial Ground*, 1851. (Via Google Books).

Brooks, Paul. *The Old Manse and the People Who Lived There.* Carlisle, MA: Applewood Books, 1983.

Citro, Joseph A. *Cursed in New England: Stories of Damned Yankees.* Guilford, CT: Globe Pequot Press, 2004.

D'Agostino, Thomas. *Passing Strange: True Tales of New England Hauntings and Horrors.* New York: Mariner Books, 1997.

———. *Abandoned Villages and Ghost Towns of New England.* Atglen, PA: Schiffer Publishing, 2008.

———. *Haunted Massachusetts.* Atglen, PA: Schiffer Publishing, 2007.

East, Elyssa. *Dogtown: Death and Enchantment in a New England Ghost Town.* New York: Free Press, 2009.

Forest, Christopher. *Boston's Haunted History: Exploring the Ghosts and Graves of Beantown.* Atglen, PA: Schiffer Publishing, 2008.

Goodwin, Nicholas. *Spooky Creepy Boston*. Atglen, PA: Schiffer Publishing, 2010.

Hawthorne, Nathaniel. *Mosses From an Old Manse*. New York: G. P. Putnam's Sons, 1846. (Via Google Books)

Hughes, Patricia. *More Lost Loot: Ghostly New England Treasure Tales*. Atglen, PA: Schiffer Publishing, 2011.

Huiginn, E. J. V. *The Graves of Myles Standish and Other Pilgrims*, 1892. (Via Google Books).

Muise, Peter. *Legends and Lore of the North Shore*. American Legends. Charleston, SC: History Press, 2014.

Nadler, Holly Mascott. *Ghosts of Boston Town: Three Centuries of True Hauntings*. Camden, ME: Down East Books, 2002.

Peterson, Pam Matthias. *Marblehead Myths, Legends and Lore: From Storied Past to Modern History*. Charleston, SC: History Press, 2007.

Revai, Cheri. *Haunted Massachusetts: Ghosts and Strange Phenomena of the Bay State*. Haunted Series. Mechanicsburg, PA: Stackpole Books, 2005.

Schechter, Harold. *Fatal: The Poisonous Life of a Female Serial Killer*. New York: Gallery Books, 2009.

Snow, Edward Rowe. *Boston Bay Mysteries and Other Tales*. New York: Dodd, Mead, 1977.

———. *Mysterious Tales of the New England Coast*. New York: Dodd, Mead, 1961.

———. *The Islands of Boston (Massachusetts) Harbor, 1630 to 1971*. New York: Dodd, Mead, 1971.

Soini, Wayne. *Gloucester's Sea Serpent*. Charleston, SC: History Press, 2010.

Yankee Magazine. *Mysterious New England*. Compiled by Austin W. Stevens. Hopkinton, NH: Yankee Books, 1971.

Zwicker, Roxie. *Massachusetts Book of the Dead: Graveyard Legends and Lore*. Charleston, SC: History Press, 2012.

MULTIMEDIA

The Bridgewater Triangle. Blu-ray/DVD. Produced and directed by Aaron Cadieux and Manny Famolare. Bristol County Media/Big Operations Productions and Flib Productions, 2013. 10 Stonewall Avenue, Dartmouth, MA 02747.

NEWSPAPER/WEB-BASED ARTICLES

Annear, Steve. "A Lincoln Field, a Herd of Hobby Horses, and a Whimsical Mystery," *Boston Globe*, September 4, 2015.

Beck, Karen. "852 Rare: Old Books, New Technologies, and 'The Human Skin Book' at HLS," Harvard Law School Library Blog, April 3, 2014. http://etseq.law.harvard.edu/2014/04/852-rare-old-books-new-technologies-and-the-human-skin-book-at-hls/

"Bound in Human Skin," Houghton Library Blog, May 24, 2013, http://etseq.law.harvard.edu/2014/04/852-rare-old-books-new-technologies-and-the-human-skin-book-at-hls/http://blogs.law.harvard.edu/houghton/2013/05/24/bound-in-human-skin/.

Driscoll, Anne. "Castle is Inventor's Vision of the Past," *New York Times*, October 9, 1988.

"Ghouls, Ghouls, Ghouls: Pervy Pole-Tergeist Interrupts Pole Dancing Classes," Caters News Agency, catersnews.com/stories/latest-news/ghouls-ghouls-ghouls-pervy-pole-tergeist-interrupts-pole-dancing-classes.

Hageman, William. "Lizzie Borden, Animal Lover," *Chicago Tribune*, September 30, 2014.

"History of the Boston Subway," *Boston Globe*, boston.com/news/globe/ideas/gallery/first_big_dig

Hubbard, Jeremy, and Jake Whitman. "Historians Study Forgotten Tombs under Boston's Oldest Church," abcnews.go.com, April 23, 2009.

"Husband Guilty in Slaying," *New York Times*, November 8, 1996.

Jacobs, Samuel P. "The Skinny on Harvard's Rare Book Collection," *Harvard Crimson*, February 2, 2006.

Kandarian, Paul. "Paying Late Respects," *Boston Globe*, April 15, 2012.

MacNeil, Arianna. "Proctor's Ledge in Salem Confirmed as Witch Execution Site." The *Salem News*, January 11, 2016.

"Man Charged with Desecrating Corpse from Civil War-Era Tomb." Associated Press, August 26, 2005.

Marx, Walter H. "Boy in the Boat Statue." *Jamaica Plain Gazette*, August 3, 1989. (Via the Jamaica Plain Historical Society, www.jphs.org)

"Mental Patient Held in Dismemberment Murder," Associated Press, Wednesday August 13, 1980.

Myers, Jennifer. "For 10 Years, 'Jolly Jane' Poured Her Poison," *Lowell Sun*, November 2, 2011.

Plumb, Taryn. "'Bridgewater Triangle' Film Cites Litany of Mysteries," *Boston Globe*, May 4, 2014.

———. "Ghost Hunting Offered at Havehill College," *Boston Globe*, January 29, 2012.

"The Remarkable Confession of Nurse Jane Toppan: Admits to Killing Thirty-One Persons," *New York Times*, June 25, 1902.

Ryan, Andrew. "Mayor Menino at Home Away from Home," *Boston Globe*, January 13, 2013.

"The Science of Anthropodermic Binding," The Houghton Library Blog, June 4, 2014. http://blogs.law.harvard.edu/houghton/2014/06/04/caveat-lecter/

Sullivan, Mark. "Decades Later, the Dover Demon Still Haunts," *Boston Globe*, October 29, 2006.

"Teeners Report 'Creature,'" Associated Press, May 16, 1977.

"Volume Bound in Human Skin Included in Miniature Collection," *Harvard Crimson*, February 16, 1933.

WEBSITES

Biography.com, "Black Dahlia Biography," biography.com/people/black-dahlia-21117617.

The Boston Athenaeum, bostonathenaeum.org.

Boston Fire Historical Society, "Fire Story: The Cocoanut Grove Fire," bostonfirehistory.org/firestory11281942.html.

"Boston Firsts," cityofboston.gov/visitors/about/firsts.asp

The Cambridge Department of Public Works, "Old Burial Ground," cambridgema.gov/theworks/ourservices/cambridgecemetery/oldburialground.

"The Cocoanut Grove Fire," a project of the Cocoanut Grove Coalition, cocoanutgrovefire.org.

Danvers State Insane Asylum, danversstateinsaneasylum.com.

Danvers State Memorial Committee, dsmc.info.

"Dighton Rock: Its Museum and its Park" dightonrock.com/dightonrockitsmusuemanditspark.htm.

Federal Bureau of Investigation, "Famous Cases and Criminals: The Brinks Robbery," fbi.gov/about-us/history/famous-cases/brinks-robbery.

Forest Hills Cemetery, foresthillscemetery.com.

Forest Hills Educational Trust, foresthillstrust.blogspot
.com/2010/02/little-grace-allen.html.

Gypsy Rose Dancing, gypsyrosedancing.com.

Hammond Castle, hammondcastle.org.

Kirkbride Buildings, kirkbridebuildings.com.

Lizzie Borden Bed and Breakfast, lizzie-borden.com.

Lowell Cemetery, lowellcemetery.com.

Mass Drive Blog, blog.massdrive.com/2012/10/haunted-
drives-across-the-bay-state.

"Metropolitan State Hospital," Lexington Historical Commission, historicsurvey.lexingtonma.gov/lexareas/
area_aa.htm.

Mount Auburn Cemetery, mountauburn.org.

National Park Service, "North Bridge Questions," nps.gov/
mima/north-bridge-questions.htm

The New England Ghost Project, neghostproject.com.

Odd Things I've Seen, oddthingsiveseen.com.

"People and Events: The Murder of Dr. Parkman," *American Experience*, PBS, pbs.org/wgbh/amex/murder/
peopleevents/e_murder.html.

Press, Margaret (author of mysteries and true crime),
margaretpress.com.

Public Health Museum, publichealthmuseum.org.

Stoughton Historical Society, "The Namesake of Stoughton,
Massachusetts . . . William Stoughton." stoughton
history.com/williamstoughton.htm.

Veasey Memorial Park, veaseypark.org.

ABOUT THE AUTHOR

Taryn Plumb is a freelance writer based outside of Boston whose topics have ranged from ghosts and goblins to the intricacies of finance (which subject frightens you more?). She has always had a fascination with the paranormal.